FAITH UN...

A Story of Transformation and Faith

Huai Man Cing

Editing, cover and author services by Opulent Books:

www.OpulentBooks.net

First Printing, 2024

ISBN: 978-1-916691-12-4

Dedication

This book is dedicated to my late mother, Cing Khan Ciin, a woman whose firm faith was a light throughout my spiritual journey.

Cing Khan Ciin was more than just a mother to me, she was a spiritual guide and mentor. During the times when my faith wavered, when I grappled with doubt, it was her gentle encouragement that led me back to prayer. Her faith was unshakeable, and it was this resolute belief in the power and love of God that she continually urged me to hold onto.

Her support for my ministry was strong. Even as her time on earth was drawing to a close, and I was away tending to the spiritual needs of others, her words were a source of comfort and strength. "Do not stop your ministry because of me," she would say, "I will be in heaven. You do not need to worry." Her absolute certainty in God's promise of eternal life was inspiring and continues to motivate me in my ministry and faith journey.

Her faith was cultivated from a young age and it was from this deep, solid foundation that she guided me towards God. When I sought a deeper connection with God, she pointed the way, and this guidance was pivotal in my own journey of faith.

This book is proof of her faith and the incredible legacy she left behind. Cing Khan Ciin was a faithful servant, her spiritual courage and passionate prayers have left a lasting impact, influencing the course of my own faith journey.

So, this book is for her, in honor of her faith in God, her steadfast encouragement, and her unconditional love. Her example continues to guide me, her faith continues to inspire me, and her love continues to strengthen me.

May this dedication be a fitting tribute to a remarkable woman and the permanent mark she left on my faith journey. As I continue to walk the path of faith, I carry her legacy with me, inspired by her faith, her commitment to prayer, and her beautiful spirit.

Table of Contents

Introduction

My journey begins in a place far removed from where I stand now, in terms of geography, mindset, and spirit. I was born and raised in Burma, now known as Myanmar, a Southeast Asian country nestled between India and Thailand.

This book traces my personal transformation, the kind that goes beyond mere physical or mental change, the kind that reaches deep into the core of your soul and alters it. This transformation started with a challenge. A challenge not from the world, but from within me. The Christian God is a living God, right? This thought troubled me. I could not continue worshipping a God I was not sure existed. I needed a personal encounter, a Divine affirmation that He was indeed real.

Coinciding with my spiritual search was my pursuit of a medical degree. I worked hard, diligently preparing for my entrance exams. However, three months into my sabbatical from the church, life took an unexpected turn. I was paralysed, a healthy aspiring student one moment and a bedridden patient the next. I found myself confined to a hospital bed. Doctors were left bewildered, unable to diagnose my condition.

My faith was shaken, yet a glimmer of hope surfaced amid the despair. I was reminded of my challenge to God. If He was real, this was the moment to reveal Himself. I yearned for a Divine intervention, a signal that I was not alone in this ordeal. And then, it happened just two weeks into my paralysis, God healed me. I will write more about that in the pages to come. My faith journey truly began in that miraculous moment.

This book is my story, a recounting of Divine

encounters that have transformed my life. If not for God's love for me, my story could have been radically different. My purpose is to share my experience and the lessons I have learned. By doing so, I hope to inspire Christians, especially those questioning the existence or power of God, to deepen their faith. I want to illustrate through my life that God is indeed alive and that He can be encountered in every situation, be it in sickness, difficulties, or moments of joy.

This story will be told as though we are engaged in a heart-to-heart talk, sharing my spiritual experiences. In sharing my story, I hope to reinforce the fact that our faith is not just about rituals or idols. It is about the personal encounters and relationships we develop with God. I pray that as you delve into my story, you will not merely be reading a tale, but living through the experiences, the trials, the triumphs, and the transformations along with me.

As we journey together through these pages, I invite you to question, reflect, and explore your relationship with God. I want you to see how the Living God touched my life when I was paralysed, both in body and spirit and how He lifted me out of my despair and led me to a life of service. It is my hope that my experiences can be a beacon to those navigating their own dark nights of the soul, affirming that even in our deepest despair, we are never alone.

In reading my story, I hope that you too will experience the Living God, whether for the first time or in a deeper, more profound way. I hope you will see how the Divine encounters I had shaped my life, gave me strength to bear difficult situations and sickness and helped me overcome my struggles.

My prayer is that you will find courage and inspiration in my story. Whether you are at the peak of your faith or in doubt, remember that God is alive and eager to have a personal relationship with you. I hope my journey encourages you to delve deeper into your faith, experience the living God in your own life, and emerge transformed.

No matter the uncertainties that cloud your way, there

is a living God who knows you by name and who is always with you. This book will inspire you to unveil your own faith, to embrace the Divine encounters waiting for you. I want to thank my husband and four children for supporting me on this journey of my life. Welcome to my journey—a story of transformation and faith. Let us unveil the power of faith together.

Chapter 1

My Life Before Christ

Born into a family of six siblings, I am the youngest. Tragically, we lost a brother and a sister at a tender age, further tightening the bonds between the remaining four of us. My father served as a police officer, a demanding job that saw our family move frequently. This nomadic life meant that our religious grounding was somewhat unstable. Whilst my grandparents worshipped spirits, adhering to animistic beliefs, my parents, especially on my mother's side, leaned towards Catholicism.

I was twelve when tragedy struck our home. My father, my hero, the one I looked up to, was suddenly taken ill. His illness was perplexing, with doctors unable to diagnose the cause. For two weeks, we watched him suffer, and then, as swiftly as the sickness had come on, we lost him.

The Salvation of Mum and Dad

Just two days before my father's passing, an incident occurred that was nothing short of miraculous. Deacons, friends of my father, sensed the urgency of his condition and came to his side. Our family had been praying for his salvation, and these deacons took it upon themselves to guide my father through his final spiritual journey.

As a police officer, my father had judged countless criminals, and this weighed heavily on his conscience. He wrestled with the thought: "How could God ever accept someone like me?" Yet, as the deacons ministered to him and led him in a confession of his sins, my father surrendered his life to Jesus. Even as a child, playing nearby, I could not ignore the profound transformation taking place. Tears streamed down my father's face as he gave his life to Christ, speaking of a vision, perhaps of heaven, which brought him immense peace. Two days later, he was gone.

This pivotal event marked the beginning of our family's spiritual reawakening. Witnessing my father's salvation, my mum felt an urgent need to dedicate her life to Jesus. She often referred to the scripture about the "narrow way," emphasising that few find it but it leads to eternal life. Not long after my father's passing, my mum too committed her life to the Lord.

Our relatives, staunch Catholics, could not understand our family's newfound faith. They pressured my mum to abandon her beliefs, especially since our Baptist congregation forbade the sale of alcohol, a potential source of income for a widow. They urged her to return to the Catholic fold and earn a livelihood by selling alcohol. But my mum's faith was unwavering. "Even if we go hungry or face death," she declared, "our trust is in God, not man."

Miraculously, our once barren garden started yielding bountiful crops after my mum prayed over it. From maize to cucumbers to pineapples, our produce became renowned for its exceptional taste, providing us with a sustainable income. It was evident that God's hand was upon us.

Years later, after I graduated from Bible College and became a pastor, one of my cousins, who had once discouraged my spiritual path, sought reconciliation. He acknowledged the success of my ministry and expressed his pride. It was a testament to God's work in our lives.

Reflecting on my father's last moments, I now understand the significance of his salvation. At the time, I felt God had not answered our prayers for healing. But witnessing my father's spiritual rebirth, I realised that the salvation of the soul is far better than physical healing. God answered My prayer in different way by giving him salvation. As it is mentioned in John 12:24 (NIV), *"Very truly I tell you, unless a grain of wheat falls to the ground and dies, it remains only a single seed. But if it dies, it produces many seeds.*" Just as a seed must die to bring forth life, my father's spiritual transformation planted a seed of faith in our family, leading us all to salvation.

It is Never Too Late for Salvation

Witnessing my father embrace Jesus Christ at the brink of his earthly journey profoundly shaped my spiritual perspective. I became passionate for personal evangelism. It instilled in me a fervent belief: it is never too late for salvation.

For many, the end of life is a time of reflection, a juncture where life's choices converge and the soul seeks peace. While some find solace in memories, others grapple with unresolved matters of the spirit. It is this crucial juncture that has become my mission.

Inspired by my father's eleventh-hour salvation, I have developed a deep compassion for those nearing life's end. I believe that everyone deserves the chance to find the same peace and redemption that my father did. Regardless of the life one has led, the blood of Jesus Christ can bring unparalleled peace and assurance as one prepares to transition from this world.

My mission is to ensure that others, too, get the opportunity to know Jesus and experience the profound peace He offers, even in their final hours. After all, it is not about how or when we start our spiritual journey, but where it leads us in the end.

The story of the thief on the cross is a powerful testament to the idea that it is never too late for salvation. Found in the Gospel of Luke, this narrative unfolds during the crucifixion of Jesus.

As Jesus was crucified between two criminals, one of them mocked Jesus, challenging Him to save Himself and them. However, the other criminal rebuked the mocker and acknowledged his own guilt, stating that they were getting what their deeds deserved, but Jesus was innocent. He then turned to Jesus and said, "Jesus, remember me when you come into your kingdom."

Jesus replied, "*Truly I tell you, today you will be with me in paradise.*" Luke 23:42-43 (NIV)

This brief exchange emphasises that, even in his final moments, the thief recognised Jesus as the Messiah and expressed genuine repentance. Jesus' response assures us of His boundless mercy and the promise of salvation. The thief on the cross did not have the opportunity to be baptised, lead a righteous life, or do good deeds, yet his faith in that crucial moment granted him eternity with Jesus.

This story serves as a profound reminder that it is never too late to turn to God and receive salvation. No matter how much time has passed or what one has done, God's grace and mercy are always available.

No matter where you have been, what you have done, or how far you feel you have strayed from God's path, there is always a way back. The story of the thief on the cross is not just a story; it is evidence of the limitless grace and mercy that God extends to all of us. You are not too far gone, and it is never too late. God's love is unconditional, and He waits with open arms for you to seek Him. Just as the thief's sincere faith in his final moments led him to salvation, your sincere faith can lead you to the same. Remember, with God, every moment is an opportunity for a new beginning.

Passion For Medicine Ignited

As the youngest, I had always been daddy's girl. Every day after school, like clockwork at four in the afternoon, I would eagerly run to meet him as he finished his day at the office. It was our special moment, a routine that brought immense joy to my heart. His sudden departure left a gaping hole in my life. I felt lost, bereft, as though my entire world had crumbled.

His mysterious illness and passing ignited a passion within me. I was determined to understand medicine, to probe into its details, and perhaps find answers to the questions that plagued our family. I knew that pursuing a medical career would be challenging and would require top marks in school. Motivated by my father's memory, I immersed myself in my studies. By God's grace, I excelled academically, setting me on a path towards achieving my goal.

In the midst of my academic pursuits, however, I was still searching for something more profound, something to fill the void left by my father's departure.

Early Encounter with Church

My first introduction to church was through my elder sister's friend. This friend had invited her to Sunday school, and after attending, my sister returned home with sparkling eyes and an excited heart. "It is wonderful," she exclaimed, and her enthusiasm was so infectious that she soon had her two sisters, including me, accompanying her the following Sunday.

I remember my first day at Sunday school clearly. The story of Daniel in the lion's den was the lesson of the day. The story of faith, courage, and Divine intervention fascinated me. I was captivated not just by the story, but also by the way it was conveyed. The Sunday school teacher, with her captivating storytelling, made a lasting impression on me. I thought to myself, "I wish to tell stories just like her one day." This early experience sowed the seeds of passion in me, leading me to conduct youth camps and Sunday school lessons in later years. The importance of a dedicated Sunday school teacher who can profoundly impact children's lives became evident to me. That's the power of a story well told.

Reflecting upon this, I have come to realise the significance of sowing seeds in young hearts. Even if they do not immediately embrace faith, planting that initial seed of curiosity and wonder can make all the difference. Each Sunday thereafter, I eagerly awaited the stories. At that time, my primary draw to Sunday school was the pull of these Bible stories, rather than a deep spiritual calling. Every story, every lesson, was like a seed being planted, laying the foundation for the faith that would later grow within me.

Where is God?

By the time I was 16, my spiritual journey had progressed. No longer confined to a youth group, I found myself attending a larger church, a step up from the storytelling sessions I had become accustomed to. Here, the focus shifted from stories to proper worship. During services, I would hear the constant mention of 'God'. This repetition sparked a curiosity within me; I began to wonder, "Where is this God they speak of?"

Looking around, I saw deacons and men leading the service, but no clear representation of the deity they referred to. My intrigue grew; I yearned to understand and connect with this elusive entity.

Growing up in a diverse community, I was familiar with various religious practices. Buddhism, with its statues in temples, was a religion I often encountered. I had seen worshippers bring flowers and water as offerings to these statues during festive occasions. And though my family did not practice Buddhism, attending these festivals with friends offered me a glimpse into their rituals.

My maternal family, largely Catholic, had its own set of rituals. Visiting their churches, I had seen figures of Mother Mary cradling the infant Jesus, statues that provided a tangible representation for worshippers. It made sense to me; there was a figure, an image, something tangible to focus on.

However, the Baptist church was different. There were no statues, just an image or perhaps a cross. It was devoid of any physical representation of God. This left me pondering, "Who or what do they worship?"

The absence of a clear icon or image made me question the very essence of worship in the Baptist faith. My young heart and mind grappled with this concept, yearning for clarity and understanding.

I Stop Going to Church

The more I attended church, the more I found myself grappling with the question: "Where is God?" Initially, I thought my curiosity was an isolated feeling, unique to me.

But as the days turned into weeks, a nagging unease settled within me. My spirit yearned for a deeper understanding, a tangible connection.

To be candid, there were moments when sitting in church felt like a lost cause. Every second spent there seemed like a missed opportunity, particularly with my ambition to excel in the medical field. The thought persisted: wouldn't those two hours be better spent studying? This reasoning grew stronger, providing a convenient excuse to distance myself from church.

One day, I voiced my doubts to my mum. "Where is God? Why cannot we see Him like Buddhists see Buddha or Catholics see Mother Mary in statues?" My mum, ever patient, explained that God is Spirit, not bound by a physical form, but ever-present for those who believe. "Even if Buddha is there as a statue," she reasoned, "he has a mouth, nose, and eyes, yet he cannot see or speak. God, though unseen, is very much alive." My mum, could not read the Bible, yet, she knew the Word through the Spirit of God.

Despite her comforting words, my doubts increased. "Until I experience God as real," I declared, "I will not attend church." My mum, heart heavy with concern, respected my decision. She could not compel me to believe. I learnt later that she had called my sisters and their prayer group, urging them to pray for my return to faith.

For a time, I diligently used those church hours for studying. It seemed like the right decision, but little did I know the path God had laid out for me and the profound experiences that awaited.

The Bible's Stand Against Idolatry

The Bible underscores the essence of genuine worship in the teachings of Jesus. In His conversation with the Samaritan woman at the well, Jesus emphasised that true worshippers will worship the Father "in spirit and truth." This profound declaration underscores that worship is not merely an external ritual, an idol or a tradition to be followed. Instead, it is a heartfelt, genuine connection with God that transcends physical locations, objects or ceremonial practices. God is Spirit.

"God is Spirit, and those who worship Him must worship in spirit and truth." John 4:24 (NKJV)

The verse from Exodus is one of the Ten Commandments, foundational laws given by God to Moses on Mount Sinai for the Israelites. It emphasises monotheism and the exclusive worship of the LORD, the God of Israel. This commandment warns against the creation and veneration of carved images or any representation of God. The underlying message is the unique and incomparable nature of God. The mention of God being a "jealous God" signifies His desire for exclusive devotion from His followers.

"You shall have no other gods before Me. You shall not make for yourself a carved image—any likeness of anything that is in heaven above, or that is in the earth beneath, or that is in the water under the earth; you shall not bow down to them nor serve them. For I, the LORD your God, am a jealous God." Exodus 20:3-5 (NKJV)

The verse from 1 Corinthians, penned by the Apostle Paul to the church in Corinth, underscores the same theme but in a New Testament context. The city of Corinth was known for its diversity and had influences from various religions and cults that practised idol worship. Paul's admonition to "flee from idolatry" was a call to the early Christians to avoid any practices or rituals that could compromise their devotion to Christ. In essence, while the cultural and historical context differs, the core message remains consistent: the worship of the one true God.

Together, these verses span the Old and New Testaments, highlighting the Bible's consistent stance against idolatry and the importance of undivided worship of God.

"Therefore, my beloved, flee from idolatry." 1 Corinthians 10:14 (NKJV)

A Serious Health Challenge

Living in Chin State, a hilly region in Burma, came with its own set of challenges. Unlike the plains, this area was defined by its biting cold, a stark contrast that often caught its residents off guard. As exam time drew near, I devised a unique strategy to keep myself awake during those long nights of study. In a bid to ward off sleep, I would dip my feet into cold water buckets, to maintain the chilling sensation. My singular focus was on achieving distinctions in my exams, a requirement to study medicine, my dream.

This nightly habit, however, had grave consequences. After three months of this routine, I found myself paralysed from the waist down. My nerves felt frozen, unresponsive to any stimuli. Even when doctors pricked me with needles, I felt nothing – no pain, no sensation. It was as if the lower half of my body had frozen.

Just three months prior, I had declared my need for a tangible encounter with the living God before returning to church. And now, here I was, immobilised, while my peers sat for their exams.

This ordeal was not just a physical trial; it was a profound spiritual lesson. Often in my testimonies, I recount this revelation: no matter our capabilities, intelligence, or preparations, it is God who dictates the course of our lives. I was ready for the exam, both mentally and physically. Yet, when the day came, I was incapacitated. My dreams, ambitions, and hard work were useless at that moment. It was a stark reminder that human efforts, lacking God's blessing, often falls short. In my weakest moment, I realised that true strength and success come from aligning our desires with God's will.

From my waist down, there was a chilling numbness. Doctors tried different tests, even using needles, but I felt nothing. It was as if the lower half of my body had turned to stone. Strangely, just three months before this, I had voiced my doubts about attending church unless I truly felt the presence of the living God. And then, in what felt like the blink of an eye, I was paralysed and confined to a hospital bed. While my peers were taking their exams, I was left grappling with my situation, unable to join them.

This period brought me face-to-face with a profound spiritual lesson. Every time I share my story, I stress one key message: no matter how smart, prepared, or capable we think we are, without God's blessing, our plans mean nothing. I was ready for my exams, confident in my knowledge and preparation. Yet, I was not able to take them. It was clear that God had other plans for me.

The lesson was unmistakable: while we can prepare and plan, it is God who determines our path. Our efforts, without His guidance, often fall short. This was a humbling time for me, a moment that deepened my faith and understanding of God's grand design for each of us.

"*In their hearts humans plan their course, but the LORD establishes their steps.*" Proverbs 16:9 (NIV)

This verse from Proverbs tells us something simple but deep. We all make plans. We think about what we want to do next and where we want to go. But, at the end of the day, it is God who decides what happens.

In my life, I saw this happen. I worked hard and was ready for my exams. I had big dreams of becoming a doctor. But then, I could not move half my body. Suddenly, everything changed. It seemed like God had other ideas for me.

The Sovereign Hand of God

"Many are the plans in a person's heart, but it is the LORD's purpose that prevails." Proverbs 19:21 (NIV)

God's power is vast and all-encompassing. Whether we recognise it or not, He is always in control. We might think we are steering our own ship, and making our own choices, but in reality, we are moving within the path He has laid out for us. It is easy to forget that even when we are busy making plans, setting goals, and chasing dreams, God's hand is guiding us. His control is not just over our lives but over the entire universe, from the vast galaxies to the tiniest plants on Earth.

I learnt this in a deeply personal way. I had plans. I had prepared diligently for my exams, confident in my abilities and my future. I envisioned myself taking the exams, passing with flying colours, and heading off to university. But God had other plans. It was not that I took the exam and failed. It was that I never even got the chance to sit for it. It felt like a door had closed before I even reached it.

This experience was a stark reminder: our plans are just that, plans. It is God's purpose that ultimately unfolds. It is a humbling realisation, but also a comforting one. Knowing that an all-powerful God is guiding our steps, ensuring we are where we need to be, even if it is not where we thought we would be.

What this teaches us is the importance of trust and surrender. While it is natural to make plans and have ambitions, it is equally crucial to acknowledge God's sovereignty, and to understand that His plans are bigger and often better than ours. Our role is not to dictate our path but to walk in faith, trusting that God's purpose for us, no matter how unexpected, is always for our good.

God's sovereignty ensures that He has a purposeful plan for each one of us. This plan, beautifully articulated in Jeremiah, is one of prosperity, hope, and a promising future. Our destiny is not just an abstract concept; it is a

Divine appointment that has been set in place by God Himself. Yet, while this destiny is preordained, our journey towards it requires our conscious choice to align with God's will. If we stray from His path or choose not to embrace His plans, we risk distancing ourselves from the very destiny He has crafted for us. Jeremiah's words serve as a poignant reminder: while God has a vision for our lives filled with hope and promise, it is up to us to actively seek and walk in His plans to truly realise our God-given destiny.

"For I know the plans I have for you," declares the LORD, "plans to prosper you and not to harm you, plans to give you hope and a future." Jeremiah 29:11 (NKJV)

Purpose, Plan, and Interruption

When we look at the story of Adam, we are introduced to a being created in God's own image, meant to be an ambassador or representative of God on Earth. The Garden of Eden was a manifestation of perfection, a place where every conceivable need was met. God's purpose for

Adam was clear, and He provided a plan in alignment with that purpose.

Adam had the freedom to enjoy every fruit in the garden, symbolising the vast array of choices and blessings available to him. However, there was a single prohibition: the fruit of the tree of the knowledge of good and evil. This singular restriction represents the boundaries set by God, not to limit human enjoyment, but to protect humanity from harm.

Adam's choice to eat the forbidden fruit, despite having countless other options, is reflective of the human tendency to gravitate towards the very things we are cautioned against. It is an inclination to challenge boundaries, even when everything we need and more is already within our reach. This act was a deviation from God's plan, leading to consequences that reverberate to this day.

Similarly, in our lives, God has a purpose for each of us and a plan to achieve that purpose. Like Adam, we are often placed in environments where most choices lead to blessings, but there are specific actions or paths that can lead us astray. Knowing our purpose is not enough; we must also adhere to God's plan to achieve that purpose. Any deviation, often influenced by external temptations or internal desires, can derail us from our Divine destiny.

The enemy, in his mission to divert us from God's plan, often magnifies the allure of the forbidden or tempts us to stray from the righteous path. Recognising these distractions and realigning ourselves with God's plan is crucial. The story of Adam serves as a poignant reminder: while we are recipients of God's purpose, it is our responsibility to choose the right path and stay true to the Divine plan.

Throughout biblical history, we see a recurring theme: the lives of God's chosen often face interruptions—unexpected events or challenges that seem to derail them from their destined path. Yet, in the grand plan of God's design, these interruptions often serve a Divine purpose, moulding characters, testing faith, and ultimately aligning destinies.

Take, for instance, Joseph. His life was marked by significant interruptions. From being sold into slavery by his own brothers to being unjustly imprisoned in Egypt, his journey seemed to diverge dramatically from the dreams of greatness he had as a young boy. However, each interruption was a step towards fulfilling a larger purpose. His time in Potiphar's house, his interpretation of dreams in prison, and his eventual rise to power in Egypt were all instrumental in preserving the Israelites during a time of famine. What appeared as setbacks were, in fact, setups for God's plan to unfold.

David, the shepherd boy destined to be king, faced his share of interruptions too. Before he could ascend to the throne, he was pursued by a jealous King Saul, faced internal strife within his family, and navigated the challenges of leadership during times of war. Yet, each challenge refined his character, tested his faith, and prepared him for his role as the king after God's own heart.

These stories illuminate a profound truth: human logic is fallible. Our perceptions of setbacks, delays, or interruptions are limited. While our human understanding might view these events as obstacles, in God's omniscient view, they are often necessary detours, shaping us for the roles we are destined to play.

Thus, the lesson that resonates through these narratives is the unreliability of human judgment in the face of Divine wisdom. While human plans might be well-intentioned, they are not infallible. It is only when we surrender to God's guidance, trusting Him through the interruptions, that we align ourselves with His perfect purpose and plan.

Let us read an example from the Bible:

"Balaam got up in the morning, saddled his donkey and went with the Moabite officials. But God was very angry when he went, and the angel of the Lord stood in the road to oppose him..." Numbers 22:21-22 (NIV)

The story of Balaam in the Bible is a powerful reminder

of how God sometimes interrupts our path when we are headed in a direction that is not aligned with His will. Balaam was on his way to meet Balak when an angel of the Lord stood in his path. The donkey he was riding on could see the angel and refused to move forward. Balaam, oblivious to the angel's presence, became frustrated and beat the donkey. It was only when the Lord opened Balaam's eyes that he saw the angel and understood the Divine interruption.

Similarly, in my life, I believe that my health challenges were a "Divine Interruption" from God. He wanted me to stop, reflect, and turn my attention to Him. From my experience, it is not always about debating or negotiating with God during these interruptions. It is about how we react and what we learn from them. The key is total surrender.

God had placed me in the perfect environment to encounter Him. This happened through my sister and our shared church experiences but I had resisted.

In Genesis 3:8-9, is one of the earliest and most profound stories of human defiance against God's will. God had given Adam and Eve the freedom to enjoy everything in the Garden of Eden, with one exception: they were not to eat from the tree of the knowledge of good and evil. However, influenced by the serpent's deception, Eve, and subsequently Adam, chose to eat the forbidden fruit.

Their act of disobedience not only led to a direct violation of God's command but also brought sin and its consequences into the world. Realising their error, Adam and Eve felt shame and tried to hide from God, illustrating humanity's instinctive reaction to distance ourselves from the Divine when we have done wrong.

I tried to distance myself, going my own way. I felt lost. If I had continued on that path, I might have faced even greater challenges. I am deeply grateful that God intervened early in my journey. It was not until I was confined to a hospital bed, with time to reflect and nothing to distract me, that I truly surrendered to Him.

If things are not going as you planned, instead of resisting or fighting the current, it might be time to pause and surrender. This is the message I want to share. When we keep resisting God's plans, it might take us longer to truly encounter Him and understand His purpose for our lives. It is in surrendering that we find clarity, purpose, and a deeper connection with God.

The Garden Theology: The Cross in Eden

In the verdant surroundings of the Garden of Eden, a story unfolds, one that hints at the larger narrative of mankind's redemption. Genesis chapter five paints a picture of Adam, created in God's image. Yet, after the events surrounding the forbidden fruit, the narrative takes a turn. Adam and Eve, having faced the consequences of their disobedience, bring forth another son, Seth. But the scriptures say Seth was born in the likeness of Adam, not God. This subtle yet profound distinction underlines the shift from the Divine to the earthly, a lineage now tainted by the aftermath of sin.

But even in this moment of profound disruption, God's Divine plan was already taking shape. The enemy might have thought he had triumphed, ensnaring Adam and Eve in his web of deceit. But God, in His infinite wisdom, had already set the wheels of salvation in motion. This becomes evident in Genesis 3:15, where God, addressing the serpent, proclaims, "And I will put enmity between you and the woman, and between your offspring and hers; he will crush your head, and you will strike his heel." This prophetic statement, nestled right there in the heart of Eden, hints at the formation of the cross. The 'crushing' and 'striking' depict the battle between good and evil, with a promise of eventual victory. This "crossing out" by the offspring of the woman suggests the symbolism of the cross, a beacon of salvation.

So, right there, in the Garden of Eden, amidst the very first act of rebellion, the shadow of the cross looms large. Salvation was not an afterthought; it was embedded in the very fabric of creation. God's intention to redeem, restore, and reconcile humanity to Himself was unwavering. The garden, where the seeds of sin first germinated, was also the very ground where the roots of redemption began to spread.

Asking God For Help

"Ask, and it will be given to you; seek, and you will find; knock, and it will be opened to you." Matthew 7:7 (NIV)

Asking God for help, in line with the verse from Matthew 7:7, is pivotal because it acknowledges our dependence on a higher power. When we ask, it signifies our humility, recognising that we do not have all the answers. It also strengthens our relationship with God, drawing us closer to Him. By seeking His guidance, we open ourselves to Divine wisdom and intervention, ensuring that our paths align with His purpose for our lives. In essence, asking God for help not only brings solutions to our immediate concerns but also deepens our spiritual bond with Him.

At 17, when life was supposed to be carefree and filled with dreams of the future, I found myself confined to a hospital bed, unable to move. The doctors, with all their knowledge and expertise, could not diagnose my condition. It was as if my body had locked up, yet inside, my mind and spirit were swirling in a storm of confusion and desperation.

I remember those nights, the stillness of the hospital room only interrupted by the distant beeping of machines and the soft murmurs of night-shift nurses. In those quiet moments, I started speaking to God, perhaps for the first time sincerely. "God, if You are real, if You are there, show me. Heal me," I would whisper, tears rolling down my cheeks.

But even in my desperation, I was stubborn. As loved ones came to pray for me, I would often turn them away. Not out of pride or anger, but from a deep desire to know God for myself. I did not want to lean on the faith of others, no matter how genuine their prayers were. Like the paralysed man whose friends brought him to Jesus, I wanted a direct encounter, not one mediated through the faith of others.

I shared my feelings with my mother. "Mum," I said, "I do not want to worship your God. I want to find Him for myself." I knew many people attended church and followed religious rituals because of family traditions. But I did not want that. I yearned for a personal relationship, a direct connection with the Divine.

In hindsight, I see how God was working even in my stubbornness. He was drawing me closer, making me thirst for His presence. And it is this thirst, this desperate longing, that I believe He responds to.

For anyone reading this, my message is simple: Seek God for yourself. Do not rely solely on the faith of others or the traditions passed down to you. While these can guide and nurture you, a personal encounter with God is what truly transforms and heals.

The Strength of Collective Prayer

Prayer is a powerful force. Even when I was deeply set in my ways, resistant to the prayers of those around me, the strength of their faith persisted. It is strange; I wanted to rely solely on my faith, feeling it was a journey I needed to walk alone. Yet, looking back, I see the power of prayers made by my church's youth group, my sister's prayer circle, and even the prayer group my mother established at home. They might not have been at my bedside, but their voices echoed in the heavens on my behalf.

Though I was stubborn, not wanting to admit the importance of others' prayers, their spiritual intercession never ceased. I was blinded by my doubts, consumed by uncertainties.

God's presence is a constant. He is always reaching out, waiting for us to grasp His hand. Yet, my own inner battles acted as a veil, clouding my vision. It was the combined strength of prayers from those who cared for me that finally tore this veil apart, allowing the light of God's love to shine through.

The wisdom in Matthew 5:8 says, "*Blessed are the pure in heart, for they shall see God.*" My heart was not pure; it was weighed down by doubt and overshadowed by pride. It was the prayers of others that acted as a purifying fire, refining my faith and enabling me to truly see and feel God's presence.

In essence, while personal connection with God is vital, the prayers of a community act as a safety net, catching us when we fail. In the next chapter, I will share a special moment that changed my life forever. It is a story about how God's love truly works in amazing ways. Get ready to hear about a real-life miracle.

Chapter 2

A Miraculous Encounter

Lying in that hospital bed for two weeks felt like forever. Each day blended into the next, marked only by the constant hum of my thoughts and the distant sounds of the ward. On one particular Thursday morning, something extraordinary happened.

It was around 4am. The hospital, being in a remote area, did not have regular electricity. We depended on lamps for light, but at that early hour, everything was covered in darkness. In the midst of this quiet, I heard a

Voice. Soft, gentle, distinctly male. It called my name. At first, I thought I was dreaming, but the clarity of the Voice made me sit up in surprise.

I looked around, expecting to see a doctor or nurse, but there was no one. The ward was still, covered only in the dim light of the early dawn. The Voice called out to me again, this time with more urgency. It was not just calling my name; it was telling me to sit up, to respond.

I was stunned. Here I was, in a nearly pitch-black room, hearing a voice with no clear source. It was mysterious, but comforting. The third time the Voice spoke, it felt like a gentle push, guiding me towards something greater than I could understand at that moment.

This was just the beginning of an encounter that would shape the rest of my journey.

A Miraculous Healing

There I was, lying on my bed, unable to even wiggle my toes. But this Voice, gentle yet insistent, was encouraging me to move three times. Despite the logical part of my brain reminding me of my paralysis, a strange sensation began to bubble up inside of me. It felt like a tingling in my spine, a warmth spreading down to my legs. They felt heavy, yet alive, as if they were waking up from a long slumber.

I called my sister, who had been by my side throughout this ordeal and asked her to help me sit up. She looked at me, disbelief clear in her eyes, and murmured, "You must be dreaming. Remember, you are paralysed." But I was insistent. There was a feeling, like pins and needles, coursing through my legs. It was as if blood was flowing into parts of me that had been lifeless for so long.

With some hesitation, she finally helped me up. And to our amazement, I sat upright on the bed. By the next day, I was slowly moving my legs. Two weeks later, I was standing and then walking, much to the astonishment of everyone around me.

The hospital staff were baffled. Every time a doctor or nurse came to check on me, I would excitedly share my experience. "I heard a Voice," I would tell them. "It was God, the Father, calling out to me, urging me to move." Their reactions were mixed, but one thing was undeniable: a miracle had taken place. "It must be real," some of them mused, "You were paralysed just last night, and now you are moving."

Within a fortnight, I left the hospital, walking out on my own two legs. The experience had transformed me. I felt a deep connection with God the Father and was eager to share my miraculous story with anyone who would listen.

Divine Healing

Many people argue that Divine healing is not for today. However, I stand as evidence to the contrary – I am a product of a miracle. God is very real. If you are reading this and you, or someone close to you, need healing, here are a few verses to reassure you that God wants to bring healing to you:

1. **Exodus 15:26** - "He said, 'If you listen carefully to

the Lord your God and do what is right in his eyes, if you pay attention to his commands and keep all his decrees, I will not bring on you any of the diseases I brought on the Egyptians, for I am the Lord, who heals you.'"

2. **Psalm 103:2-3** - "Praise the Lord, my soul, and forget not all his benefits— who forgives all your sins and heals all your diseases."

3. **Isaiah 53:5** - "But he was pierced for our transgressions, he was crushed for our iniquities; the punishment that brought us peace was on him, and by his wounds, we are healed."

4. **James 5:14-15** - "Is anyone among you sick? Let them call the elders of the church to pray over them and anoint them with oil in the name of the Lord. And the prayer offered in faith will make the sick person well; the Lord will raise them up."

Remember, it is never too late, and you are never too far gone for God's healing touch. Hold onto these promises and believe in His power to restore. If you need healing in your body, please pray this prayer.

Healing Prayer

Heavenly Father,

I come before you, seeking your healing touch for the one reading this or for their loved one. By the power of Jesus' sacrifice, I ask for restoration. Let every pain, illness, and discomfort be replaced with health and vitality. May they feel your presence and be reassured that you are with them in this moment. Increase their faith, Lord, and let them experience the fullness of your healing love.

In Jesus' name, Amen.

God the Father

Upon reflection, while my physical recovery was undeniably miraculous, an equally real transformation was taking place within me. There was a deep-seated recognition, a sort of spiritual feeling, that assured me the voice I heard was that of God the Father.

The concept of God as a Father is woven throughout the Bible, painting a picture of His character and attributes. God the Father embodies compassion, love, protection, and guidance. As a Father, He seeks the best for His children, guiding us through the trials and tribulations of life, much like a loving parent would. His love is unconditional, not based on our actions or worthiness but simply because we are His children.

Moreover, God the Father is a protector. Just as earthly fathers would go to great lengths to ensure the safety and well-being of their children, God watches over us, shielding us from harm and providing refuge in times of distress.

While I had experienced the love and healing of the Father, my spirit sensed there was more to this Divine relationship. Intuitively, I knew I had not been born again; I had not yet met the Saviour who would bring about a deep and transformational change within me. I needed salvation, not just healing.

The concept of the Trinity, though complex, became real to me during this time. I had encountered God the Father, felt His immense love and power, but I yearned to know Jesus, the Son. The Father had shown me grace and healing, but I now sought salvation and redemption – gifts only Jesus could provide.

The Trinity At Work

At its core, the Trinity is the belief that God exists as three persons - God the Father, God the Son (Jesus Christ), and God the Holy Spirit - yet is one God. This is not a matter of three gods, but rather one God in three persons, each distinct, yet fully God.

God the Father is the first person of the Trinity. He is often depicted as the creator, the source of all life, the one who set the universe into motion. In my experience, I related most closely to Him as a loving parent, guiding, protecting, and speaking tenderly to me during my most vulnerable moments. (Genesis 1:1, 1 Corinthians 8:6)

Jesus Christ, the Son, is the second person of the

Trinity. He is God incarnate, God in human form, who lived among us, taught us, suffered, died, and was resurrected for our salvation. Through Jesus, we see the Father's love in action, manifested in a tangible way that we, as humans, can relate to. (John 1:14, John 3:16)

Lastly, the Holy Spirit, the third person of the Trinity, acts as our guide, comforter, and advocate. The Spirit dwells within believers, guiding our steps, convicting us of our wrongs, and empowering us to live according to God's will. (John 14:16-26)

"Go therefore and make disciples of all nations, baptising them in the name of the Father and of the Son and of the Holy Spirit." Matthew 28:19 (NIV)

In this verse, Jesus instructs His disciples to baptise believers in the name of the three persons of the Godhead: the Father, the Son, and the Holy Spirit. This highlights the concept of the triune nature of God, which is foundational to Christian belief.

Just a few months after my miraculous healing, my

spiritual hunger grew even stronger. I was not content with just knowing God as my healer; I wanted to know Him in His fullness. The idea of God as a healer was comforting, but I wanted more. I wanted to be reborn, to experience a new life in Christ, to truly be a child of God.

My journey led me to countless prayers, seeking encounters, and yearning for a deeper connection with Jesus. And as days turned into weeks, my perseverance bore fruit. The experience of being 'born again' is hard to put into words. It is a deep inner transformation, a feeling of being renewed from the inside out.

In retrospect, I see how God, in His infinite wisdom, introduced Himself to me in stages, each encounter designed to draw me closer to Him. From the Father's healing touch to the saving grace of the Son, and ultimately, the comforting guidance of the Holy Spirit, I came to understand and embrace the mystery of the Holy Trinity.

There is a yearning inside all of us, a void that seeks to

be filled. For me, it was a longing for salvation, a connection with my Saviour. I had encountered God the Father, but I knew in my heart that I had not been born again. I was hungry for more!

Chapter 3

Meeting The Lord Jesus

The air was electric, a palpable energy vibrating through the crowd. It was at a revival crusade that I had been invited to attend. This was two months after my healing encounter with God the Father. It was a week-long event, filled with sermons, worship, and countless testimonies of salvations. Many, including my sisters, were moved by the Lord Jesus and dedicated their lives to the Lord.

However, as each day passed, I felt distant. The final evening arrived, and while the air was thick with Gods power, my heart remained unyielding. I participated in the rituals, sang the hymns, and listened intently to the sermons. But a nagging doubt held me back, preventing me from fully accepting Jesus as my personal Saviour. Perhaps it was my naturally analytical nature, my need for proof, or just a deep-seated scepticism. I did not want to commit merely to satisfy others or to fit in; it had to be genuine, a true calling from within.

That night, as we returned home, my mother, with a mix of concern and confusion, asked, "The crusade is over. You have not given your life to Christ. What's holding you back?"

I sighed, searching for the right words. "Mum, I am still seeking. I need to be certain in my heart. Just... pray for me."

With that, we retired for the night, each lost in our thoughts, hoping and praying for clarity and guidance in the days to come.

A Visit from the Lord Jesus

That night, everyone else was fast asleep, but not me. I was just lying there, wide awake. And then, around 11 o'clock, something extraordinary happened. I saw Jesus, sitting right at the corner of my bed. Just like how I recognised God the Father a few months before, in that moment, I immediately recognised Him. It is Jesus – God the Son. We did not exchange words, but it felt like our spirits were communicating, you know?

Now, here is what really got to me. With Jesus right there, I started seeing myself in a new light. I always thought of myself as a good person. I mean, I never indulged in stuff like smoking or drinking. I never got into any immoral relationships. But with Him sitting there, I felt... different. Not as righteous as I thought. It was like there was a mirror in front of me, but instead of reflecting my face, it showed all my imperfections, my inner flaws.

In that moment, I did not know all the fancy terms or

deep theological stuff, but I felt this sense of "original sin". It is not just about doing good things or avoiding bad habits. It was deeper than that. There is this gap, this distance between where I am and where He is. That night was not just a casual encounter. It was a wake-up call, showing me that I had so much more to learn and a long way to go in my spiritual journey. It showed Me how much I needed God as a Saviour in my life.

Original Sin

"Therefore, just as sin entered the world through one man, and death through sin, and in this way death came to all people, because all sinned." Romans 5:12 (NIV)

The concept of "original sin" is rooted in the story of Adam and Eve in the Book of Genesis. When they disobeyed God by eating the forbidden fruit, sin entered the world. Romans 5:12 captures this idea by stating that sin came into the world through one man, referring to Adam, and as a result, death (both physical and spiritual) came to all of humanity. In essence, because of Adam's disobedience, all of us inherit a sinful nature from birth. This does not mean we are guilty of Adam's sin, but rather that we are born with a propensity to sin. It is a spiritual condition that underscores our need for redemption and salvation, which is provided through Jesus Christ.

Think about a dog. Whether it barks or remains silent, it is inherently a dog by nature. Similarly, take a mango tree. Whether it bears fruit or stands barren, its inherent identity as a mango tree remains unchanged. In much the same way, the concept of Original Sin underscores a fundamental truth about human nature. Regardless of our deeds, whether good or bad, or our successes and failures in life, the imprint of original sin remains. Our actions, no matter how noble, cannot erase this inherent condition. As the scripture says, "*Behold, I was brought forth in iniquity, and in sin my mother conceived me*" Psalm 51:5 (NKJV). This intrinsic state of sin, ingrained in our very being from birth, underscores our profound need for a saviour. It is not our deeds, but this inherent nature, that necessitates salvation.

The Power of Jesus' Blood

"In him we have redemption through his blood, the forgiveness of sins, in accordance with the riches of God's grace." Ephesians 1:7 (NIV)

As I was having communion with the Lord Jesus. He did not utter a word, but we did not need words. There was this profound spiritual connection, a silent communication. It felt as though our spirits were entwined, and I could grasp what He wanted to convey. It was an indescribable moment. I was flooded with awareness – an overwhelming realisation of my imperfections and sinful nature.

I saw the power of the Blood! The enormity of my sins weighed heavily on me. And as I sat there, feeling so unworthy and so small, something incredible happened. From the cross, I saw droplets of blood fall – the blood of Jesus. It felt as if each drop was washing away a part of my sin, purifying me. It was not just a physical cleansing but a profound spiritual one.

Then, enveloped in this newfound purity, I felt the embrace of the Father God. But it was not just me and Him. Jesus was there, bridging the gap. It was a communion, a union so intimate and profound. I was in Jesus, and through Him, I was with the Father. That moment ignited something I would later find in the scriptures: Jesus, the mediator, the bridge to our reconciliation with the Father.

In the silence of that moment, the words of 1 Timothy 2:5 seemed to echo in the chambers of my heart: "For there is one God and one mediator between God and mankind, the man Christ Jesus." This scripture illuminated the profound reality I was experiencing.

Jesus stood as the bridge, the sole connector, drawing me into the embrace of God the Father. It was through Him, through His sacrifice and His eternal role as a mediator, that I could feel this deep communion with the Divine. This was not merely about redemption; it was an ongoing, ever-present intercession, a continuous linking of my soul with the Creator.

This revelation deepened my understanding of Jesus's role. He was not just the Saviour who had redeemed me from my sins; He was the eternal conduit allowing me to experience the warmth, love, and intimacy of the Father. Through Him, my relationship with God was not just restored but intensified, becoming a communion so profound that words could barely capture its essence.

Born Again

I was born again that night! Praise the Lord! I was wrapped in His grace, covered head-to-toe with His blood. The real Jesus set me free, and through Him, I saw not just Him but also God the Father. It was an embrace so liberating that any chains, doubts, or fears simply melted away. I felt like I could soar. It was like I was on the edge of taking flight. Everything was so clear, so pure. Did I sleep? Honestly, I cannot even remember.

By dawn, the world looked different. The flowers in my garden? They sparkled with a beauty I had never seen before. And as I watched people pass by my home, my heart ached for them. They were walking, unaware of the great price Jesus paid for them. I felt a burden, an urgency to reach out.

From that day on, I began to perceive things differently. I sensed burdens, felt diseases, and had a supernatural awareness. It was like discernment or a Word of Knowledge had been implanted in me. When I step into church, I could sense the spiritual journeys of those around me. During that period, I sometimes even knew if someone was nearing the end of their life. Relatives would often come to me, seeking prayers for their ailing loved ones or asking if it was time to share the Gospel with them.

What I am trying to convey is how transformative that night was for me. My entire being – my spirit, my soul – was reborn. I had tapped into the spiritual realm in a way I had never thought possible. My life changed for good. If God can do it for me He can do it for you.

The Trilogy of My Spiritual Awakening

My transformative journey unfolded in three distinct

stages, each one deepening my connection to God and reshaping my understanding of faith.

Firstly, there was my encounter with God the Father. It was He who called out to me, drawing me close in my time of vulnerability and healed me. His voice, gentle yet profound, beckoned me, and I felt His presence in ways I could never articulate. It was a tender embrace, a fatherly love that I had never known.

Then came my meeting with the God the Son who is Lord Jesus Christ. It was an encounter that shattered my perceptions and rebirthed my spirit. Through Jesus, I understood the weight of my sins, the gravity of the original sin, and the cleansing power of His sacrifice. The blood of Jesus did not just cleanse; it transformed. I felt reborn, made anew, ready to live my life with purpose and conviction.

And finally, the guidance of God the Holy Spirit took centre stage. From that transformative morning, my very being changed. My perspectives shifted, and my spiritual senses were heightened. The Holy Spirit led me, guiding my every step, providing discernment, and unveiling the truths of the spiritual realm. I was not just living; I was being led.

These three encounters, with the Father, the Son, and the Holy Spirit, shaped the trajectory of my spiritual journey. It was a trinity of experiences, each one leading me deeper into the heart of God. I am going to be talking about the Holy Spirit in the next chapter.

A Call to Action

If you have read my story to this point and felt the stirrings in your heart, and sense a yearning deep within, know this: God's love and transformative power is not just for a select few. If He could reshape my life, breathe purpose into my existence, and lead me to a profound understanding of His love, He can and will do the same for you. If you are searching and want give your life to the Lord Jesus – this is a good place to do so.

Perhaps you are reading this and thinking, "Could God

really have a plan for me? After everything I have done, is there truly a place for me in His embrace?" The answer, my dear reader, is a resounding YES. His arms are open wide, waiting for you to take that step, just as I did.

If your heart is calling out, if you desire to experience the same love and transformation I did, I urge you to say this prayer with me:

Prayer of Salvation

Dear Lord Jesus,

I come to You today, acknowledging that I am a sinner in need of Your saving grace. I believe that You died on the cross for my sins and rose again, victorious over death. I ask You to forgive me of all my sins, known and unknown. Wash me with Your precious blood and make me clean.

Today, I declare that You are my Lord and Saviour. I surrender my life to You. Come into my heart, lead me, and guide me on the path You've set for me.

Thank you, Jesus, for accepting me, for loving me

unconditionally, and for promising me eternal life with You. Fill me with Your Holy Spirit, that I may walk in Your ways and live a life pleasing to You.

In Jesus' name, I pray. Amen.

Next Steps

1. **Find a Local Church**: Seek a local church where you can grow in your faith, learn more about God's Word, and be part of a community that will support and encourage you.

2. **Read the Bible**: Start with the New Testament, perhaps the Book of John. It will help you understand the love of Jesus and His teachings.

3. **Pray Regularly**: Make it a habit to talk to God daily. Share your joys, fears, and ask for guidance.

4. **Seek Fellowship**: Join a Bible study group or fellowship where you can discuss your experiences and learn from others.

5. **Share Your Testimony**: Just as you have read

mine, share your story with others. Your testimony could be the beacon of hope for someone else.

Remember, God's love for you is boundless. If He could transform my life, He can certainly do wonders with yours. Embrace this new journey with hope, faith, and a heart full of gratitude.

Chapter 4

Embracing The Holy Spirit

Just like a baby needs milk right after being born, once we are born again in our faith, we need more. We need the Holy Spirit. Think about a baby looking for milk, never giving up until they get it. The Bible even talks about this in 1 Peter 2:2 (NIV), saying, *"Like newborn babies, want the pure milk that will help you grow and be saved."* In this chapter, we'll learn why the Holy Spirit is like that milk for our hearts and how to truly welcome Him into our lives.

With the life-changing experience of meeting God the Son, something shifted within me. The Holy Spirit, that powerful presence of God, took residence in my heart. Yes, I felt His touch when I was saved, but there is a depth to the Holy Spirit many of us do not seek out or even realise exists.

In that profound moment, it felt like God the Father, Jesus, and I were beautifully woven together, a bond so tight and unbreakable. This unity opened my eyes in ways I had never imagined. The world looked different, and God's presence was more tangible than ever. It was not just a fleeting feeling; it was the tangible manifestation of the Holy Spirit.

The Holy Spirit did not just show me God; He gave me new eyes and a new heart. I was given the gift of inner knowledge. With it came a kind of spiritual clarity, a new lens through which to view life and its challenges. But, with this newfound clarity, I also faced a challenge. I realised I had two distinct voices guiding my decisions. One voice was from my logical mind, my head, often influenced by the world around me. The other voice, pure and guiding, came from my heart, the dwelling place of the Holy Spirit.

This duality presented me with choices each day. Which voice would I listen to? Which path would I follow? The journey with the Holy Spirit had only just begun.

But I want to put this out there for anyone feeling content with just being 'born again': Do not stop there. Picture a newborn baby. Once they are brought into this world, they do not just lie there, satisfied with birth. They cry, they seek, they long for milk to grow and thrive. In the same vein, when we are spiritually reborn, it is the start of a journey, not the end.

Now, with the Holy Spirit within me, my perspective changed. I no longer saw the world or God in the same light. This change, this enlightenment, was the manifestation of the Holy Spirit's work. I was not just looking through my human eyes; I was discerning with spiritual eyes. Suddenly, every day was a choice: Would I listen to the voice in my head, led by fleshly desires, or would I tune into the voice in my heart, guided by the Spirit?

This duality, these two natures battling within, became evident. It reminded me of the biblical sisters, Mary and Martha. Martha busied herself, eager to serve, while Mary chose to sit at Jesus' feet, listening and learning. Every morning, I face a similar choice: Do I rush into the day, catering to my human desires, or do I first sit in God's presence, seeking His guidance? Believe me, the choice I make sets the tone for the entire day.

So, to all reading this, I urge you: Do not settle at the 'born again' stage. Continue to search, to seek, and to be led by the Holy Spirit. Do not let the flesh dominate; let the Spirit guide. The journey with the Holy Spirit is ongoing, and every step is worth it.

How to Identify Whether It is Your Mind or Your Heart

Oh, discernment! It is a journey, is not it? Distinguishing between the voice of our own minds and the gentle nudges of our heart – where the Holy Spirit often speaks – can be a real puzzle. But over time and with practice, we can get better at it.

Let us take a simple, relatable example. Imagine waking up in the morning to a messy living room. Toys scattered everywhere, yesterday's newspaper spread out, maybe a leftover cup from last night's tea. Now, the mind, driven by immediate reactions, might start to boil with anger. "Why cannot they keep things tidy?" "Why is it always me cleaning up?" You might feel the urge to shout, to let out that frustration on a family member or even grumble about the weather. That's the mind, reacting instantly without pause.

But the heart? The heart, influenced by the Holy Spirit, might suggest a different approach. "Take a moment," it might whisper. "Breathe. Start the day in gratitude, not in anger." The heart seeks peace, patience, and love, even amid chaos.

So, the next time you are confronted with a situation

and feel a rush of emotions, pause. Ask yourself: Is this my mind reacting instantly, or is it the gentle guidance of my heart, influenced by the Holy Spirit?

Being led by the Spirit does not mean we will not feel emotions. We are human, after all. It means that we do not let those emotions dictate our actions or our day. Instead, we choose to listen to that still, small voice inside, leading us towards peace, love, and understanding.

Navigating between the heart and the head is a practice that requires us to embrace the Holy Spirit fully. The Bible provides wisdom on discernment, shedding light on how to differentiate between the two.

In Jeremiah 17:9 (NIV), we find: *"The heart is deceitful above all things and beyond cure. Who can understand it?"* This verse reminds us that our heart, driven by emotions, can sometimes mislead us. Emotions are powerful and can cloud our judgment if we do not view them through a spiritual lens.

On the other hand, Romans 8:6 (NIV) tells us: *"The*

mind governed by the flesh is death, but the mind governed by the Spirit is life and peace." This verse helps us understand the potential dangers of letting our minds, influenced by worldly concerns, take the lead. However, when our thoughts align with the Spirit, it leads to life and peace.

So, the question then becomes: how do we discern? It is all about our motivation and attitude. When we react out of anger, jealousy, or any other emotion, it is a burst of energy from the heart. But when we pause, reflect, and act out of love, patience, and kindness, it is the Spirit guiding us.

We should constantly check our motivations. Are we driven by personal gain, pride, or vengeance? Or are we motivated by love, compassion, and a genuine desire to do God's will?

In Ephesians 4:26 (NIV), Paul advises: *"In your anger do not sin": Do not let the sun go down while you are still angry."* It is a reminder that it is natural to feel strong emotions, including anger. However, it is crucial to not let these emotions lead us to sin.

So, it is not about suppressing our emotions or thoughts but understanding them through the lens of the Holy Spirit. Every emotion or thought can be an energy, either leading us away from or closer to God's purpose for our lives.

Discernment between the heart and the head is a continuous journey of self-reflection and alignment with the Holy Spirit. As we navigate life, let's strive to ensure our attitudes and motivations mirror the teachings of Christ, leading us closer to a life filled with love, peace, and purpose.

Rediscovering Purpose Through the Word

After that intimate encounter with Jesus, the world as I knew it shifted. The appeal of a career in medicine, which once held such a grip on my heart, started to fade. It felt like I had outgrown an old passion, and it no longer resonated with the direction my soul was taking. Instead, a new hunger took root, an unquenchable thirst for the

Word of God.

Before I met Jesus, reading the Bible often made me sleepy. But after that special encounter, the Bible felt different. It was like it woke up, full of life and meaning. You see, without the Holy Spirit, the Bible can seem hard to understand. But with the Holy Spirit's guidance, every word shines brightly, making sense and touching the heart. Now, every time I read, it is like going on a new journey with the Holy Spirit showing me the way.

You see, it was not just about reading the Bible; it was about immersing myself in it, understanding it, letting its truths seep into every corner of my being. Every verse I read seemed to call out to me, speaking directly to my soul. It was so captivating that moving from one verse to the next became a slow, meditative process. The Word was no longer just words on a page; it was alive, vibrant, and deeply personal. It felt like God was speaking directly to me through each passage.

I remember those days so vividly, holding my Bible

close, not wanting to miss a single revelation. The pages of Scripture became my daily bread, nourishing my spirit, providing clarity, and lighting up the path ahead. It became evident that God had a different journey mapped out for me, one that went beyond the confines of a clinic or hospital. He was leading me into a deeper understanding of Him and a renewed purpose that I had never anticipated.

The Bible itself speaks volumes about the importance of reading and meditating on the Word. As I delved deeper into my own spiritual journey, I was reminded of Psalm 119:105 (KJV), "*Your word is a lamp to my feet and a light to my path.*" It is incredible how the words written thousands of years ago were still so relevant, guiding my steps and illuminating the challenges and decisions I faced daily.

Moreover, Joshua 1:8 (NIV) further cemented the importance of immersing oneself in Scripture: "*This Book of the Law shall not depart from your mouth, but you shall meditate on it day and night, so that you may be careful to do according to all that is written in it. For then you will make your way prosperous, and then you will have good success.*" It was clear that meditating on God's Word was not just a mere exercise; it was a directive, a path to success and prosperity in every aspect of life.

The more I leaned into these truths, the clearer it became that my relationship with the Word was not just about knowledge; it was about transformation. It was about allowing God's Word to reshape my thoughts, desires, and actions. Every time I opened the pages of the Bible, I was not just reading; I was engaging in a Divine conversation, one that had the power to change the very core of my being.

My Bible Study Regime

My Bible study routine might seem a bit distinct, but it is deeply personal and has been transformative for me. The Bible is not just a book I read; it is the sustenance for my soul, the very bread that nourishes my spirit.

Every time I open the Holy Scriptures, it is like preparing for a meal. I do not just dig in. I start by dedicating myself – my ears to hear, my eyes to see, and most importantly, my heart to understand. It is a little ritual I have adopted. No one taught me this; it felt instinctual, perhaps a gentle guidance from the Holy Spirit. Before going into the Word, I would often pray, "Lord, speak to my heart. Let me see what you want me to see in these pages. Let your truth resonate in me."

And when I read the Gospels, oh, it is like embarking on a journey. I always ask the Lord to walk me through the footsteps of the Apostles – Matthew, Mark, Luke, and John. Why? Because they had the privilege of walking with Jesus. They witnessed His teachings, His miracles, and His love firsthand. So, in my mind's eye, as I read, I follow them. I imagine being right there, alongside them, experiencing the stories as they unfold. It is not just reading; it is living the Word. Every story, every parable, feels alive, feels real.

This approach changed the way I connect with God's Word. It is no longer a passive act of reading but an immersive experience, one that draws me closer to Jesus with every page I turn. Try it.

The Spirit of Truth

One of the vital roles of the Holy Spirit is to lead believers into all truth. This is especially important when studying the Bible, as the Scriptures are divinely inspired, and having the Holy Spirit's guidance ensures that one accurately interprets and understands God's Word.

The Gospel of John has a clear reference to this role of the Holy Spirit:

"When the Spirit of truth comes, he will guide you into all the truth, for he will not speak on his own authority, but whatever he hears he will speak, and he will declare to you the things that are to come." John 16:13 (NIV)

This verse underscores the Holy Spirit's role as the "Spirit of Truth." When Jesus spoke these words, He was assuring His disciples that after His ascension to heaven, He would send the Holy Spirit to guide, teach, and remind them of everything He had taught. For believers today, the Holy Spirit continues this role, illuminating the Scriptures and providing insight into God's character and His plans for humanity.

This guidance from the Holy Spirit is what ignites a hunger for biblical truth in believers. When you have experienced the transformative power of God's Word, coupled with the illuminating presence of the Holy Spirit, there is an insatiable desire to delve deeper, to understand more, and to align one's life more closely with God's will. It is not merely about acquiring knowledge, but about deepening one's relationship with the Lord and understanding His heart more clearly. The Holy Spirit, acting as a guide and teacher, ensures that this journey into the depths of Scripture is accurate, enlightening, and life-changing.

I want to stress the importance of the Holy Spirit in our walk with God. If you truly desire to walk in step with God, it is essential to fully embrace the Holy Spirit and yield to His transformative power. He is not just a silent witness; He actively guides, teaches, and moulds us, aligning our hearts with God's purpose. My own life stands as a testament to this. The direction of my journey was profoundly shifted by God, and it was the Holy Spirit that clarified the path I needed to take. As we go into the next chapter, I will show you how God redirected my steps and the incredible journey that followed.

Chapter 5

My Encounter With The Holy Spirit

In the Book of Acts, the apostles got the Holy Spirit and started speaking in other languages.

"And they were all filled with the Holy Spirit and began to speak in other tongues as the Spirit enabled them." Acts 2:4 (NIV)

But for me, a person who always approached things with logic and reason, the concept of speaking in tongues was hard to understand. It seemed too abstract, too beyond the realm of the tangible.

During college, I loved to pray. I would spend all night in the prayer room talking to God. But some people, especially my dorm leaders, did not like it. They would sometimes lock the prayer room door, and sometimes they even locked me out.

But I kept praying. After some time, though, their actions made me feel less and less like praying. It made my heart feel heavy. Funny thing was, the same people who tried to stop me from praying later had problems. They got sick or had bad things happen to them. And guess what? They came to me asking for prayers.

When I prayed for them, and they got better, it showed me something big. The Holy Spirit's gifts are real and strong. No one can stop them. Those college years taught me a lot about the power of the Holy Spirit.

My Visit To Heaven

In November 1988, I was leading a week-long seminar on the foundations of the Christian faith. We had many newcomers, and as we journeyed through the teachings, I felt a deep connection with them. They were so appreciative of my sessions that they offered me various drinks and food in gratitude. Unbeknownst to them, and certainly to me, something I consumed had been contaminated, and I fell victim to food poisoning.

Three days into the seminar, the effects of the food poisoning took a severe toll on me. I was rushed to a hospital, but my memories of that time are hazy. What I do remember is slipping into a coma. But even in that unconscious state, I experienced something ineffable - a visit to heaven.

While my physical body lay in a hospital bed, surrounded by grieving family and friends, my spirit felt liberated. I found myself in the presence of the Lord in heaven, and it was an overwhelming feeling of joy and peace. The sights and sounds were beyond description. I remember seeing a choir of angels, their voices harmonising in a melody that seemed to resonate through every fibre of my being. Their chorus of "Hallelujah, Holy" was so pure, so divine, that when I tried to join in, my voice felt out of place, lagging behind their celestial harmony.

Wondering why my voice could not match theirs, I was filled with knowledge - without anyone saying a word, I understood. The Lord conveyed to me that it was not my time yet; I was not ready to be part of that heavenly choir.

But then came a moment I will never forget. Jesus approached me, affixing a beautiful badge upon me, inscribed with His name. He then gave me what felt like a Divine mandate. With a touch, almost like a 'high five', He sent me back with a mission: "Heal the sick and set the captive free."

Even now, when I recall this experience, it fills me with a sense of purpose and clarity. The memory serves as a reminder of the Divine task entrusted to me, and of the love and power of the Saviour.

After my return from heaven, I opened my eyes to see my family right by my side. Their eyes were filled with tears, and their faces showed both surprise and relief. The pain and sickness from the food poisoning had disappeared. It was as if I had been given a fresh start.

But there was something more, something different. I soon realised I had a new ability, a special gift of discernment. I could somehow sense things before they happened. It was like having a small window into the future. One of the first times I noticed this was when I felt that people were on their way to visit me. Before anyone told me, I said to my sisters, "Let us get ready. We are going to have a lot of visitors soon." And just like I felt, many friends and well-wishers started arriving at the hospital.

This new gift was a constant reminder of the extraordinary experience I had and how God can bless us in unexpected ways.

My First Experience with Tongues

During an evangelism mission in Calcutta, India, I encountered an unusual session about speaking in tongues. At that point, I had not experienced it and was quite sceptical. Four of us from Nagaland were there, and we all had reservations about this gift of the Spirit. We were theologians, and questioning and debating were second nature to us. We brought up all our doubts, questioning the validity and relevance of speaking in tongues in our time.

Instead of debating with us, the session leader made a simple suggestion: "Let us not argue. Instead, go to your rooms and pray about it. Ask God to reveal the truth to you."

Honestly, I was reluctant. I did not want to pray about tongues because a part of me was afraid of what might happen. But I also did not want to be disobedient. So, I knelt down beside my bed in my room and began to pray. Before I knew it, my language shifted. Words I did not understand flowed from my lips. I prayed in tongues for two hours, feeling an overwhelming sense of peace and clarity.

The next morning, during our group devotion, I felt

something extraordinary. As we began to worship, it felt like I was being lifted off the ground. The atmosphere was thick with God's presence. Once again, I found myself speaking in tongues, the same unfamiliar yet comforting language from the previous night. Any doubt I had about this spiritual gift vanished.

From that moment, I began to see the importance of speaking in tongues. Whenever I faced a decision or needed guidance, I would pray in tongues, asking God for wisdom and direction. The Apostle Paul spoke about the significance of praying in tongues. He said, "For anyone who speaks in a tongue does not speak to people but to God. Indeed, no one understands them; they utter mysteries by the Spirit." 1 Corinthians 14:2 (NIV). This verse taught me that when we speak in tongues, we are communicating directly with God, uttering things our human minds might not comprehend but are understood in the spiritual realm. It is a gift that has since become precious to me, a direct line to God's heart.

The Power of Tongues in Prayer

In the early days of the apostles, as depicted in the Book of Acts, they received the Holy Spirit and began speaking in tongues.

"When the day of Pentecost came, they were all together in one place. Suddenly a sound like the blowing of a violent wind came from heaven and filled the whole house where they were sitting. They saw what seemed to be tongues of fire that separated and came to rest on each of them. All of them were filled with the Holy Spirit and began to speak in other tongues as the Spirit enabled them." Acts 2:1-4 (NIV)

When we look at the Bible, we see that speaking in tongues is a special way to talk with God. It is more than just speaking in a language we do not understand. It is a deep way to connect with God, beyond words we know. In the Book of Acts, the apostles started speaking in tongues when they received the Holy Spirit. It was a big moment for them and showed how close they were to God.

Paul, in his letter to the Corinthians, emphasised the

importance and power of speaking in tongues:

"For anyone who speaks in a tongue does not speak to people but to God. Indeed, no one understands them; they utter mysteries by the Spirit." 1 Corinthians 14:2 (NIV)

When we speak in tongues, we talk directly to God. It is a unique way of praying. For me, it changed how I pray. When I face tough times or need help, I often pray in tongues. It feels like a special way to reach out to God. So, if you are unsure about it, I would say give it a try. Let the Holy Spirit show you.

Using this way of praying has brought me closer to God. It feels like a special link between me and Him. When words cannot say how I feel, speaking in tongues helps. For anyone who has not tried it, I would say keep an open mind. Let yourself experience it. It is not about understanding everything but about feeling close to God. When you pray, let speaking in tongues help you feel that closeness.

Now, when I am faced with challenges or seeking

guidance, I often resort to praying in tongues. It has become a spiritual weapon for me. Sometimes, we need to move beyond understanding to truly encounter the Lord.

Benefits Of Speaking In Tongues

1. **Building or Edification of the Spirit**: Speaking in tongues allows for personal spiritual growth. As stated in 1 Corinthians 14:4, "*He who speaks in a tongue edifies himself...*" This means that when we engage in this form of spiritual communication, we are building up and strengthening our own spirit, nurturing our connection with God. It acts as a spiritual exercise, fortifying our inner being and drawing us closer to the Lord.

2. **Praying in God's Will**: There are times when we are unsure of what to pray for or how to express our deepest feelings and desires to God. Speaking in tongues bridges this gap. As Romans 8:26-27 explains, the Holy Spirit intervenes on our behalf when we speak in tongues, voicing out prayers that

align perfectly with God's will. The verses state, *"Likewise the Spirit also helps in our weaknesses. For we do not know what we should pray for as we ought, but the Spirit Himself makes intercession for us with groanings which cannot be uttered. Now He who searches the hearts knows what the mind of the Spirit is, because He makes intercession for the saints according to the will of God."*

3. **Sign for Unbelievers**: Speaking in tongues, also serves a crucial external purpose: acting as a sign for non-believers. The Bible references this in 1 Corinthians 14:22: *"Therefore tongues are for a sign, not to those who believe but to unbelievers..."* At its core, this means that the manifestation of tongues can capture the attention of those outside the faith, making them curious or even convinced about the Divine power at work. It is a tangible demonstration of the Holy Spirit's presence and power in the lives of believers. God often uses supernatural experiences not just to edify believers but to draw

others to Him.

Praying in Tongues for the First Time: A Guided Approach

1. **Set your tongue free**: Before venturing into the realm of speaking in tongues, it is essential to approach the experience with an open heart and mind. Let go of preconceived notions or theological barriers that might hinder your experience. It is crucial, then, to simply lay your doubts at the feet of Jesus. I remember saying, "Lord, if this is from You, I want it. If not, then I do not." This act of surrender can open doors to a profound spiritual experience.

    - Scripture Reference: Acts 2:1-4 – "And when the day of Pentecost was fully come, they were all with one accord in one place...And they were all filled with the Holy Ghost, and began to speak with other tongues, as the Spirit gave them utterance."

2. **Baby Steps**: Remember that when starting, it might not sound like fluent speech. Think of it as a baby learning to talk; they begin with basic sounds before forming words and sentences. The initial utterances might be as simple as "lalala" or another repetitive sound. It is essential not to get discouraged or over-analyse what's being spoken. Instead, embrace the process and trust that, with time and practice, the language will flow more naturally.

   - Scripture Reference: 1 Corinthians 14:2 (NKJV) – *"For he who speaks in a tongue does not speak to men but to God, for no one understands him; however, in the spirit he speaks mysteries."*

3. **Intertwine Native and Spiritual Language**: A helpful approach when trying to break forth in tongues is to start praying in your native language. As you continue in your prayer, switch between your known language and attempting to speak in tongues. This transition can sometimes act as a spiritual catalyst, allowing the Spirit to take over.

Remember, the aim is not to make logical sense but to let the spirit man communicate through you.

- Scripture Reference: Romans 8:26 (NKJV) – *"Likewise the Spirit also helps in our weaknesses. For we do not know what we should pray for as we ought, but the Spirit Himself makes intercession for us with groanings which cannot be uttered."*

In conclusion, the journey to speaking in tongues is personal and varies for each individual. Embrace the process with an open heart, and let the Holy Spirit guide your path.

Chapter 6

A Change Of Path

The Holy Spirit truly has the power to change one's mind. Before my profound encounter, my ambitions were set on a university entrance exam, hoping to secure a spot at a renowned institution. But God had other plans for me. Instead of heading to a mainstream university, I found myself drawn to a Bible College to pursue a Bachelor of Theology.

During my time there, my relationship with prayer intensified. I was constantly in the prayer room, so much so that my dorm leader would lock it, fearing I would spend all my time there. While I was devoted to my theological studies, I felt the Spirit leading me, showing me the power of healing and miracles. Interestingly, my college was not keen on these manifestations of the Spirit. However, when some of my sceptical lecturers fell ill, they'd turn to me for prayers, witnessing firsthand the miracles I had often spoken of.

Post-graduation, I returned to my home church and took up the role of a youth minister. My methods, heavily influenced by the Holy Spirit, weren't popular with the church's deacons. They weren't keen on giving me a platform. But God had other plans. A small budding church in Chin State, with only seven families, reached out to me. With the Holy Spirit's guidance, I served this church, and within a year, our congregation grew exponentially.

Looking back, I see how the Lord was moulding me for pastoral duties. My time at that church confirmed my calling to shepherd His flock. The church recently celebrated its Jubilee anniversary, a testament to its growth and the Lord's blessings. Through all these experiences, it became clear: I was destined to be a pastor, leading and nurturing the faithful in their spiritual journey.

Pastoring as a Woman

When I was just 24 years old, I took on the role of pastoring a church, even though I had no prior experience in such a leadership position. Some might wonder, "How could someone so young, without any background, lead a congregation?" The answer is simple but profound: the Holy Spirit was my guide and helper.

I did not rely on my knowledge or understanding. Instead, I leaned on the Holy Spirit every step of the way. Whenever I faced challenges or uncertainties, I would pray and seek guidance. Time and again, I felt the comforting presence and wisdom of the Holy Spirit guiding me, showing me the way forward. It was not about my skills or expertise; it was about trusting in a higher power to lead both me and the church community in the right direction.

Taking on the role of a pastor, especially as a woman, was not without its challenges. There were many who hesitated to accept a woman's voice in the pulpit. However, my approach was different. My teachings weren't just based on my studies or scripture readings. I leaned heavily on prayer, especially praying in tongues. Days before delivering a sermon, I would seek the Lord's guidance, asking Him to provide the right message for His people. I was acutely aware that only God truly knew the needs of His congregation.

And as time went on, the fruits of this approach became evident. The messages I delivered resonated deeply with the congregation, bringing about healing and transformation. It was not long before even the sceptics acknowledged the power and authenticity of my teachings. The very people who had doubts about a woman leading from the pulpit now saw the benefits of my ministry.

Despite the growth and success at the small church, the larger Baptist Church, where I had started, asked me to return. They saw the work I was doing and wanted me back. Torn between my commitment to the smaller church and the call from the bigger one, I ultimately decided to return, respecting the church's rules. But I did not leave the small church leaderless. I mentored a successor, ensuring its continued growth and spiritual nourishment.

Soon after, opportunities to teach at Bible colleges came knocking. I took on roles as a lecturer in three different institutions, balancing pastoral duties with academic responsibilities. My ministry expanded even further when I began speaking at women's conferences, starting in 2006. These engagements took me across the United Kingdom.

Today, my ministry spans teaching, pastoring, and speaking at conferences. I have also found a calling in counselling, especially in matters of family and relationships. My journey has taught me that with faith, prayer, and the Holy Spirit's guidance, barriers can be broken, and God's word can be spread far and wide.

Chapter 7

Ministry Work

After graduating from theological school, I returned home with high hopes and a heart full of passion. I had expected that my home church would welcome me with open arms, eager to make use of the knowledge and spiritual growth I had acquired. Yet, to my surprise, they labelled me "too born again" and "too charismatic." It was a stark reminder of a belief I held: It is not about where you are trained, but whom you have encountered in your spiritual journey.

The essence of our faith, our spirituality, is not determined by external factors or environments. It is an inside-out experience. While some might argue that our surroundings play a critical role in shaping our spiritual journey, I have come to realise that what truly matters is the internal transformation that takes place within us. The essence of our connection with the Lord is not about what the world thrusts upon us, but rather about the Divine presence that blooms from within.

The phrase "Inside Out" summarises this beautifully. It is not about the influences from the outside world shaping our inner selves. Instead, it is about our innermost beliefs, our personal encounters with God, shaping how we perceive and interact with the world around us.

The "inside-out" concept highlights the transformation from the Old Covenant to the New Covenant, as described in the Bible. In Jeremiah 31:31-34 (NKJV), the Lord says:

"Behold, the days are coming, says the Lord, when I will

make a new covenant with the house of Israel and with the house of Judah... I will put My law in their minds, and write it on their hearts; and I will be their God, and they shall be My people... For I will forgive their iniquity, and their sin I will remember no more."

This was a significant shift from the Old Covenant. In the past, God gave the Israelites commandments and statutes. Even though they pledged obedience, they often failed. Recognising their inability to consistently obey, God promised a new approach. Instead of external commandments, He would place His laws and commands inside their hearts, making it an "inside-out" relationship.

This profound shift is reiterated in the Book of Hebrews 8:8-12 (NKJV):

"Because finding fault with them, He says: 'Behold, the days are coming, says the Lord, when I will make a new covenant with the house of Israel and with the house of Judah... For this is the covenant that I will make with the house of Israel after those days, says the Lord: I will put My laws in their mind and write

them on their hearts; and I will be their God, and they shall be My people... For I will be merciful to their unrighteousness, and their sins and their lawless deeds I will remember no more.'"

Under the New Covenant, it is not about rules from the outside but about a relationship from the inside. With Jesus residing within us, His teachings and guidance become an intrinsic part of our being. In essence, we do not need to be continuously reminded of God's will because His teachings are already engraved in our hearts. The New Covenant underscores the importance of recognising who is inside us and living our lives from that profound connection

My principal always emphasised the importance of recognising who resides inside of us. If our inner self is empty or weak, we become soft, easily influenced by external pressures and opinions. But when our inner man is strong and rooted in faith, external environments, no matter how challenging or opposing, cannot change our core beliefs or shake our foundation. It is this inner strength and conviction that make us unyielding in the face of adversity.

So, while my home church might have been hesitant to embrace the changes they saw in me, I remained steadfast. I knew that the transformation within me was genuine, a result of my deep encounters with the Lord. And as the saying goes, when God says "yes" to you, no one else's "no" can stand in your way.

Bearing Fruit in Ministry

In many ways, the path of faith is not always about the praises or recognitions. It is about the transformation and impact you bring to those around you. There is a prevailing notion that if you do not have a solid foundation in your faith, external influences can easily sway you. But my experience was different. Despite being educated in a more liberal theological school, my charismatic convictions remained unchanged.

Upon my return, the church I once called home seemed distant. It felt as if I was in a wilderness, searching for my ministry path. But as destiny would have it, a budding group seeking to plant a new church reached out. They saw potential in me, not deterred by my youth or my gender. At just 24, I was entrusted with leading a congregation. Starting with only seven households, our numbers grew exponentially within a year. The growth was a witness not just to my leadership, but to the power of genuine faith and the Holy Spirit working through a community.

Witnessing our success, my original church reached out, hoping to bring me back into their fold. Their call was rooted in the tangible results they saw, a church flourishing under my guidance. But my heart was with the new congregation. The dilemma was real. My original church reminded me of their support, how they sponsored my education. Out of a sense of duty and gratitude, I eventually returned to them. Yet, I continued to guide and advise the new church from a distance.

The entire journey reinforced a vital lesson: It is not always about where you are or who you are with; it is about the fruits of your labour. The results of your efforts will always speak louder than words. When you genuinely bear fruit in your ministry, it becomes undeniable evidence of God's work in and through you. This fruit-bearing approach eventually paved the way for me to gain more responsibilities in my original church. I was entrusted with youth and women's ministries, and even with roles that traditionally were reserved for male leadership. It was a testament to the fact that when God's work is evident in you, barriers break and doors open.

Turning Rejection into Blessing

Experiencing rejection, especially in our spiritual journey, can be disheartening. Time and again, I found myself at the receiving end of disapproval, cast aside for my beliefs and practices. However, these rejections taught me invaluable lessons about perseverance and faith. They made me realise that sometimes, before one can truly bear fruit, they must first face and overcome numerous challenges.

Drawing parallels from the Bible, I often found comfort in the stories of Joseph and Hannah. Joseph, despite being blessed with visions, faced rejection from his own family. However, these rejections and adversities were part of God's greater plan, ensuring that the vision he held would come to fruition. Similarly, Hannah faced ridicule and sorrow because she could not bear children. Yet, in her most vulnerable moments, she turned to God, pouring her heart out in prayer. The result? Samuel, one of the most significant prophets in the Bible.

Both Joseph and Hannah faced adversities, but it is essential to understand that these trials were instrumental in shaping their destinies. The harsh environments they faced – likened to the sun, soil, rain, and air that a seed requires to grow – were necessary for their growth and eventual triumph.

The message is clear: Rejections and hardships are not always setbacks. Instead, they can be stepping stones leading us to our true purpose. Instead of harbouring resentment or bitterness, we should view these challenges as opportunities to grow and lean into our faith. By pouring our hearts out to God and seeking His guidance, we can ensure that the adversities we face do not define us. Instead, our reaction to them does.

Starting my ministry was not a bed of roses. I faced plenty of rejections and criticisms. However, these experiences only strengthened my resolve and deepened my connection with God. I learned to channel the negative energy into positive actions, consistently relying on God's wisdom to guide my steps. In the end, the results of my ministry bore witness to the strength of my faith and commitment. It is a testimony to the fact that when you stay rooted in God's love, no amount of rejection can deter you from your path.

God's Unbiased Love

In accordance with the Word of God, which unequivocally states that He is for all the people of the world, and nothing is beyond His capabilities, we understand that in His eyes, all individuals are created equal. Each person has the potential to become a child of God, entitled to the full inheritance of heaven. These Bible verses guide us on the path to love and serve everyone, regardless of age, colour, ethnicity, gender, or nationality. It is imperative to pass down these teachings to our children and future generations, fostering respect and reverence for God's love and equality for all. It is crucial to recognise that religious rules and doctrines can sometimes obstruct people from comprehending God's salvation plan for mankind. Therefore, seizing any opportunity to share the love of God becomes vital.

Jeremiah 32:27 (NLT) declares, "*I am the LORD, the God of all the peoples of the world. Is anything too hard for me?*" Furthermore, Deuteronomy 10:17 emphasises that the LORD, our God, is the God of gods and Lord of lords, displaying greatness, mightiness, and awe, showing no partiality and accepting no bribes.

In a particular instance from our own lives, my husband and I were invited to lead a child dedication ceremony for a lady from our church, who, although a church member back home in Burma, had married a Muslim husband. Despite attending church, she did not currently belong to any congregation. When she sought to dedicate her child, she faced challenges finding a church willing to accept her child due to her lack of current church membership.

Initially, I harboured scepticism about the venue when requested to lead the entire service, considering church rules and regulations. However, learning that the event would take place in a community hall eased my concerns. Reflecting on God's impartiality and acceptance of all, I convinced myself that discrimination had no place in our response. Embracing the opportunity to share the Good News with family and friends, we led the entire service and preached the Gospel to everyone present.

The Divine Connection and the Vision

My journey in ministry has been filled with unique encounters and profound experiences, and one such pivotal moment happened in 2006 when we were settled in the United Kingdom. I had been invited to a women's conference by a group I knew little about. The backstory of my invitation was nothing short of miraculous.

The Pastor's wife, seeking a change in the usual roster of speakers, took a three-day fast. On the other hand, I had been fasting for thirty days. (I will share more on fasting in the next section). During this period, she received a revelation about a minister from Burma named Sister Man. As destiny would have it, I was known by that name in my area, and I had recently joined their church in Oxford. Though our acquaintance was barely two weeks old, she recognised the Divine connection. The Lord had orchestrated our paths to intersect.

Arriving at the conference, I felt a mix of uncertainty and a linguistic challenge, considering English was not my strongest language. However, as I stood on the pulpit on the first night, the Lord provided clarity in the form of a vision. I saw Jesus, not His face but His heart, wounded and bleeding from numerous holes. As a lost soul approached and connected with His heart, the bleeding lessened, providing relief to Jesus. The message was clear: every soul that returns to Him alleviates His pain. That night, I shared the significance of having a passion for lost souls, emphasising how each one plays a part in healing the Lord's heart. The response was overwhelming, with twelve attendees committing their lives to Christ.

This profound vision deeply imprinted on my heart the importance of soul-winning. It reaffirmed my belief that every soul matters, and as ministers, we are tasked with bringing them back to the fold, back to the heart of Jesus where they truly belong. This passion for souls, ignited by the vision, continues to fuel my ministry to this day.

Prayer Cell Groups

One Friday afternoon, quite some time ago, my youngest daughter contacted me, seeking permission for her friend to spend the night at our house. After getting in touch with the girl's mother, I granted them permission to stay for the entire weekend, fostering their friendship. Throughout her stay, we maintained our regular family prayers at night. Despite her not being a Christian, we extended an invitation for her to join us during these moments. During one such prayer session, I shared the message of God's love and how Jesus atoned for our sins. On that day, she decided to give her life to Jesus Christ, and we prayed for her and her family.

Having two more daughters who occasionally stay with us on weekends, I seize opportunities, when available, to share messages of faith and minister to them. Additionally, a friend and I initiated a fasting prayer routine in the mornings, starting at 6:00 am and concluding at 8:00 am, which lasted for two weeks. Our focus during these sessions was on praying for the well-being of young people, schools, and homes.

These young girls faced significant challenges, coming from families in the midst of divorce and broken homes. Their lives were marked by isolation, and they had undergone various struggles. One of the girls was dealing with issues that led to her being detained by the school for shoplifting, while the other had turned to alcohol after school. Despite the difficulties they were facing, my daughter felt a calling to befriend them as they were often shunned by others.

Upon learning about their backgrounds, I initially hesitated and questioned whether it was the right decision to welcome them into our lives. Concerns about potential problems and uncertainties lingered. However, I chose to see them as children of God and embraced the opportunity to introduce them to their Creator, finding peace in my decision. I initiated a prayer session with my daughter and her friends, guiding them on how to connect with God. One of the girls accepted Jesus as her Saviour and Lord.

This experience prompted me to seek God's will and guidance through fasting prayer sessions with my friend. As a result, we established regular prayer cell groups in my house, meeting three times a week. Our prayers extend to young people, the well-being of the UK, and a nationwide revival. We also pray for the strength of existing churches and cover various topics as guided by the Holy Spirit.

The lessons drawn from Luke 15:1-31, Acts 2:46, Acts 16:40, Romans 16:3,5, and Colossians 4:15 collectively underscore the timeless truth that it is never too late for salvation. These scriptures reveal the inclusive love of

Jesus, demonstrating that no one is beyond the reach of God's transformative grace. The parables in Luke emphasise redemption, while the examples in Acts and the Epistles illustrate how communities, households, and even unexpected places can become centers for salvation and spiritual growth. The persistent evangelism seen in Jesus and the early Christians encourages us to persistently share the message of salvation. By grounding our ministries in the inclusive love of Christ, creating transformational communities, and using hospitality as a bridge to salvation, we can convey the powerful truth that redemption is available to all, regardless of their past or circumstances.

Fasting And Divine Direction

In 2003, after my husband completed his PhD in Glasgow University, we were all set to go back home. I was excited about seeing my family and restarting our ministry. But my husband felt we should seek God's guidance before making any decisions. So, we went for a week-long retreat.

Three days into our fasting, my husband had a vision:

God wanted us to stay in Scotland. At first, I was resistant. But after praying, I too felt God's call. Surprisingly, He revealed to me that I would study at Oxford University. This seemed impossible. I worried about my English skills and questioned the need for such an education. But God assured me that it was for a bigger purpose - to lay a strong foundation for our ministry in a foreign land.

Soon after, an opportunity arose for me to study at the Oxford Centre for Mission Studies. We moved to Oxford, expecting financial support from the Church of Scotland and the Episcopal Church. But shortly after our arrival, they withdrew their support. We were devastated, especially when our college informed us that our accommodation was available for only one more month.

During this challenging time, my husband received multiple job offers. But after accepting each, he felt they were not in line with God's plan for us. One time, after accepting a role, his car broke down, almost signaling a Divine intervention to prevent him from taking the job.

Without a job and with no financial support, we found ourselves in a dire situation. The only food in our house was some potatoes, oil, and pasta left by our landlord. It was a trying period, but we held onto our faith, believing that God had a plan.

We were forced into a fasting period, not out of choice, but out of necessity. For 28 days, we prayed intensely, seeking God's guidance. Every morning, my husband reminded me of God's past miracles, like feeding the Israelites with manna for 40 years and providing water from a rock. He believed that God would still provide for us.

On the 28th day, we received an unexpected call from David, our former landlord from our time studying in Scotland. He wanted to visit us in Oxford. Initially, I hesitated to invite him because of our situation, but he insisted. When he arrived, he shared that for two months, he had been feeling a strong call from God to support us. He had even discussed with his solicitor and daughter about adjusting his will to provide for us. David wanted to share some of his inheritance with us while he was still alive.

It was a powerful revelation. We realised that even before we faced this crisis, God had already set things in motion for our provision. It reminded us of a Bible verse from 1 Corinthians 10, which assures believers that God will always provide a way out of trials. My husband often says, "God is nearly too late, but never truly late." This experience reinforced that belief. God's provision always arrives at the right time.

After our first fasting experience which resulted in unexpected provision from our former landlord, David, I found myself led to another period of fasting. This time, it was 40 days, and during this period, I felt an intense call from God to shift my studies from my current college to Oxford University, a monumental challenge given my background.

Unexpectedly, we met a local pastor from Littlemore Baptist Church who happened to be a leader at Oxford

University's Regent's Park College. After sharing our story with her, she guided me through the application process for Oxford. Yet, the journey was anything but easy. The rigorous standards of Oxford University meant that where a pass in other United Kingdom institutions might require a 40% score, Oxford demanded 60% or higher. It was tough, but I was determined.

During the dissertation phase, I found myself overwhelmed. The task required intensive research from several books to form a cohesive theology. But I had a profound spiritual experience. One night, I felt like God was directly downloading information into my brain. The next day, as I typed, it was as if the words flowed effortlessly. When I shared my dissertation with a friend, she was amazed at the transformation in my writing.

When I submitted my dissertation, my supervisor was equally surprised. He questioned the authenticity of my work, wondering if I had copied from elsewhere. I explained that it was a Divine download, a concept he struggled to grasp. Regardless, I knew deep down that it was God's intervention that had brought me to and through Oxford.

The Lord placed me in challenging situations to showcase His might. I likened my experience to David's encounter with Goliath. I was an underdog, but I believed in the Holy Spirit's active presence and His miracles. My supervisor, initially sceptical, grew to appreciate my work. He recognised the unique touch in my writings. We maintain a connection, and recently, he revealed his cancer diagnosis to me, seeking prayers. This highlights the acceptance of the Holy Spirit's work, even in unexpected places.

I completed my studies six months ahead of my peers, an achievement achieved purely by God's grace. My journey highlighted that God always seeks willing vessels to manifest His glory. If we remain open and receptive, He uses us as instruments to touch the world.

On my spiritual journey, during a 40-day fast in 2017, the Lord empowered me with the ability to pray against cancer and sickness. I was given the declaration of being "poverty-free, cancer-free, and sickness-free." This affirmation is now a weekly declaration at the Burmese Mission Church.

By the grace of God, eight individuals diagnosed with advanced-stage cancer experienced miraculous healing. One notable testimony is the pastor's wife, diagnosed with bone marrow cancer in 2016. Through prayer, she was declared cancer-free within a short span and continues to lead a healthy life. Notably, not everyone experienced this miracle, but those whom the Lord directed me to.

Another testimony is of a former church member from outside the United Kingdom, diagnosed with cancer in 2021. She was in hospice with limited time left. Due to pandemic restrictions, I could only pray for her over the phone. After continuous prayers and taking communion, she too experienced healing.

Thus, through prayer, and fasting, I have witnessed the boundless power of God in healing and restoration. The story serves as a testament to the miracles that can manifest when we align ourselves with God's purpose.

Transformative Encounters

The Easter holiday of 2017 was one of the most successful experiences in our ministry. We were invited to Norway for the last Easter holiday for a youth Bible camp. It was a camp without outside communication. I had experienced the power of the Holy Spirit, who is greater and stronger than any other power.

There are some Burmese Christians in Norway in different parts of the country. Some of them had a burden for their children who find it very difficult to live under two cultures. They try very hard to cope with Western culture, modern lifestyle at the same time they are pressured to keep and respect our native culture. Most of their children did not know the Christian value anymore. Parents were very concerned about their children because some have been suffering from depression, and some children are influenced by different kinds of addiction. Parents were praying together regularly every week for a year. They were crying to God about how to bring up their children in a Godly way. They felt God has given them an idea of having a Bible Camp. They arranged a Youth Camp with Bible study along with games and sports in the camp. Children were very excited to play these games and sports, but they are not sure about the Bible studies.

The first night when we got there in the camp there was no internet, no telephone, no connection to the outside world. Children were a bit upset. We prayed together that night, and the Holy Spirit was at work. Most of the children were touched by the power of the Holy Spirit, and they gave their life to Jesus. They were crying and weeping with repentance from sins and dedicated their lives to be used by God. The next day they became witnesses to their friends, and they shared their experiences, and the rest of the people in the camp paid attention to the Good News of Jesus. They would like to make sure their salvation, and their relationship with God is right.

There was no time for games and sports because of the work of the Holy Spirit. No one wanted to leave Bible teaching time; they knew that it was important to know how to live a successful Christian life. It is the power of God to transform these young people when they gave their lives to God, and they did not want to play games and sport; they rather wanted to study the Bible. On Easter Sunday, they all wanted to be baptised, but there was no place available for water baptism. We told them when they got back home they can get baptised in the Church, which would be the best. However, they wanted to get baptised in the camp to make it memorable of their transforming lives so, they were baptised in the river which was full of ice under minus 5 degrees. Which was so remarkable to me the decision they had made and the strong power which influenced them was none other than the Holy Spirit.

Encountering Jesus means life-transforming experiences, as evident throughout the Bible. In John 4:4-42, the story of the Samaritan woman serves as a compelling example, resonating with my experiences during the Youth Camp. Like the Samaritan woman, who initially came to draw water for her daily needs, encountered Jesus offering living water, altering the course of her life. She abandoned her primary intention, running back to her town to witness to people she initially avoided. Leaving her water jar behind, she shared her profound experience.

The biblical account of the first disciples in Matt 4:18, Mark 1:16, Luke 5:1 further illustrates lives changed by encountering Jesus. Acts 9:1 recounts the remarkable transformation of Saul into Paul, inspiring me to boldly proclaim the Gospel, echoing Paul's words in Rom 1:16-17, "I am not ashamed of the gospel because it is the power of God that brings salvation to everyone who believes..."

These young people experienced a transformation through the power of God, facilitated by the fervent prayers of parents and leaders.

This experience gave me a new insight to encourage parents and church members to pray for our young people, that they may encounter the transforming power of God, changing the entire trajectory of their lives.

The Passing Of My Mother

I have dedicated this book to my mother - Cing Khan Ciin because her faith inspires me to this day. In 2014, at that time, when I completed my master's at Oxford University, I continued my studies at King's College in London for my Ph.D. Then, having completed the third year, I was ready to write my dissertation in the final year when my mom fell ill and was hospitalised. She does not speak English, and hiring a caregiver became challenging since she didn't understand the language. I had to feed and look after her, leading me to a struggle between continuing my studies and caring for my mom. During this time, I prayed with my family, seeking guidance. Consulting my husband, we agreed to seek the Lord's will.

Life, we concluded, does not offer repeat opportunities, but degrees and other pursuits can be achieved at different times. Recognising the temporal nature of my mother's condition, I decided to prioritise her care for this season. The dilemma arose between earning a degree and looking after my mother. In this predicament, I turned to the Lord, offering my time to care for my mother.

Consequently, I withdrew from the third year at King's College. My supervisor assured me that if I decided to resume my studies anytime within the next two to four years, I would be welcome to join. They anticipated my return after two years, assuming my mother's condition would have changed. Fortunately, by God's grace, her health improved, although she still required assistance. Two years turned into four, and I could not rejoin my studies, eventually leading to my decision to give up.

In September 2019, I was invited to a youth camp in Melbourne, Australia. The planning had started a year in advance. However, my mother's health took a downturn in September. Attempting to cancel the camp proved futile, as it was too late. Discussions with my mom revealed her supportive nature. Despite her sickness, she encouraged me to go, emphasising the importance of the ministry to young people who had yet to know God. She assured me of her certainty in salvation, providing comfort amid her impending journey to heaven.

Her encouragement allowed me to proceed with the trip, capturing a joyful moment in a photograph. She reassured me not to worry about her, expressing confidence that we would meet again. The separation was temporary, and we would be together forever.

Reflecting on her influence, I realised it was not just about her raising me but also about her encouragement to serve the Lord. Her deep and selfless faith stood out as she prioritised the kingdom of God over her health. She did not impose the expectation for me to stay and care for her but focused on the greater purpose of serving others. This perspective inspired me and became a source of strength.

While in Australia, I embarked on another ministry in Burma as part of a women's conference planned six years prior. During this time, my mother passed away. Initially, guilt overwhelmed me, but her words provided solace. She had given me permission to pursue the work of God, emphasising the Kingdom's importance over her passing. Her faith, rooted in the eternal, relieved me of guilt and allowed me to carry on her legacy.

This story underscores her as a truly born-again believer, relying on faith over worldly concerns. She inspired me to focus on the eternal and assured me of our eventual reunion. Her words continue to encourage and inspire me to this day.

Foundations of Missionary Life

Part of my work as a missionary is to minister to people I meet and tell them about Jesus. Missionary work is not only about big missions and meetings; it is about meeting people where they are. On a journey to Denver, I led a lady to the Lord Jesus who sat next to me on the plane. The Holy Spirit touched her through a cover of my book, which I was reading on the plane. The book is called 'The Word, the Name, and The Blood of Jesus,' written by Joyce Meyer.

I was invited to visit two churches in Denver, Colorado, where my sister is pastoring. One of my commitments is to share my faith and show the love of God, especially when I travel on the plane. I had done this in the past a couple of times, so I prayed that this journey would be a useful one for the Gospel. I was preparing myself to share my faith with whoever sat next to me, but it did not happen; no one sat in that row except for me.

I prayed that God would place someone next to me on my next flight who needs to hear God's love and is ready to receive the Gospel, even though it was a short journey. I was sitting with two people who were talking to each other, so I thought there was no chance to share the Gospel. I pulled out my book and started reading. A lady next to me, who was falling asleep, suddenly woke up and asked me about the meaning of the book I was reading. I had a good opportunity to share God's love and the power of the Word, the Name, and the Blood of Jesus. I explained that Jesus paid the price for our sins, and anyone who believes in Him can become a child of God and a new person. She accepted it and asked me how to pray to God. I led her and told her what to do next. She lives in Denver and helped me in the Denver airport to collect my luggage. I was so grateful to God.

My first reflection on this incident was that I learned God's way of answering our prayers could be different. He did not answer our prayers the way we want them to be. If we do not get what we ask for, it is not necessarily a negative answer. God answers our prayers in His way, which is always the best for everyone.

When one feels the call to embark on missionary work, it is easy to become overwhelmed by the sheer enormity of the task. From my experience, here is what I would advise:

1. **Inner Conviction is the Cornerstone**: Your personal calling or passion is the foundational pillar of your ministry. It should be so firmly rooted within you that external challenges will not deter you. As it says in Ephesians 2:20 (NIV), *"built on the foundation of the apostles and prophets, with Christ Jesus*

himself as the chief cornerstone."

2. **Expect Challenges and Grow from Them**: Often, the strength of your conviction will be tested. Just like a newly built pillar gets touched, tapped, and shaken to ensure its stability, you too will face challenges. However, *"Consider it pure joy, my brothers and sisters, whenever you face trials of many kinds, because you know that the testing of your faith produces perseverance."* James 1:2-3 (NIV).

3. **The Wilderness Experience**: Every missionary should prepare for their personal 'wilderness experience.' Just as Jesus went into the wilderness to fast and be tempted after His baptism (Matthew 4:1), expect challenges after you receive your calling. This period is crucial for deep spiritual growth, preparing you for the journey ahead.

4. **Understanding Your Role**: Just like John the Baptist prepared the way for Jesus, you are preparing a path for God's work. Your role might

not always be at the forefront, but facilitating and preparing for God's work is equally vital.

5. **Embrace Humility and Expect Downfalls**: Do not expect constant elevation after your calling. There will be moments of being brought low, of facing trials and temptations. This is a necessary part of the journey. As Proverbs 18:12 (NIV) reminds us, "*Before a downfall the heart is haughty, but humility comes before honour.*"

6. **It is God's Work, Not Yours**: Always remember, the ministry is not about you; it is about the Lord's work through you. Your responsibility is to remain steadfast, committed, and allow God to work through you. As Paul says in 1 Corinthians 3:6 (NIV), "*I planted the seed, Apollos watered it, but God has been making it grow.*"

7. **Be Prepared**: Finally, equip yourself mentally, spiritually, and emotionally. Dive deep into scriptures, pray fervently, and surround yourself

with a supportive community. As Ephesians 6:11 (NIV) advises, *"Put on the full armour of God, so that you can take your stand against the devil's schemes."*

In conclusion, if you are considering missionary work, ground yourself in your calling, expect challenges, and remain steadfast in your faith. The journey is tough but immensely rewarding, for *"Blessed are the feet of those who bring good news!"* Romans 10:15, (NIV)

Chapter 8

A Shared Ministry

When I returned to my local Baptist church, I was immediately involved in a youth camp that also doubled as a crusade for soul winning. Little did I know that this would be the setting where God would introduce me to my life partner. My husband was the main speaker at the event, and even though we had not met, God had already started His Divine matchmaking.

Both of us had been praying for a spouse. I had been praying for eight years, and he had been praying for ten. As

God's mysterious ways would have it, during one of the ministry sessions, without even seeing my face, God revealed to him that I was the one he would marry. But at the time, I was involved with someone else. Yet, God reassured him: "Wait, it will come."

As time passed, due to cultural norms and parental disapproval, primarily because of my health and calling to ministry, my relationship ended. As I was navigating this period of heartbreak and seeking God's direction for my future in Calcutta, my future husband approached my mother back home. My mother had a dream, which she believed was a sign from God about our union.

When I returned home, instead of a traditional love letter, he wrote to me with conviction and clarity, asking me to pray and seek God's will. At first, I was taken aback by the directness of his approach. But deep down, I felt this was a different kind of love story – one that began with spiritual alignment rather than emotional affection.

I prayed earnestly, seeking God's will above all else. I

felt a deep peace and realisation that this was God's plan. While my feelings for him were not the typical romantic kind, I trusted that God would cultivate that love in time. I asked God, "Give me a heart to love him," and He did. Our love story might not have started with butterflies and passionate feelings, but with a solid foundation of faith and purpose.

We got married with ministry in mind. We knew that our union was not just for companionship, but for a shared mission. This foundation of shared purpose ensured that our visions were always aligned, making our ministry more effective and our bond stronger.

To young people considering marriage, I often say: seek God's will first. While romantic love is beautiful, a marriage built on shared purpose and Divine alignment stands the test of time. Emotional feelings can be fleeting, but a Divine calling to be together is unshakeable.

In Proverbs 16:3 (NIV), it is written, "*Commit to the LORD whatever you do, and he will establish your plans.*" This scripture captures our love story. We committed our hearts to the Lord, and He beautifully wrote our love story, intertwining our lives in the most Divine way.

A Shared Vision

After confirming our union was in accordance with God's will, we embarked on a new chapter of our lives together. Upon marriage, I relocated to his town, aligning our paths for a shared ministry. His role as the general secretary in the association and my subsequent employment in the children's education department meant we were serving side by side, literally working in the same office.

As our ministry evolved, our roles complemented each other seamlessly. Whenever he transitioned into a new area of ministry, I found myself being divinely placed in corresponding roles that augmented his work. For instance, as he took on the mantle of the Evangelism and Mission Director, I was invited to teach at the Bible College associated with his department. This synergy allowed us to not only support each other but also amplify the impact of our collective ministry.

Growing Together

Our journey also led us to pursue further academic and theological enrichment. We moved to England, where he pursued postgraduate studies and a PhD. Simultaneously, I went deeper into theological studies, completing my master's. Our commitment to growing both spiritually and academically was a result of our shared belief in equipping ourselves for the ministry.

Currently, our roles have further evolved with him serving as an evangelist in the Baptist Union, while I shepherd a congregation as a pastor. We are both under the aegis of the Baptist Union, continuing our joint mission to spread the Gospel and serve God's people.

Ecclesiastes 4:9 (NIV) states, *"Two are better than one, because they have a good return for their labour."* This scripture resonates deeply with our journey. Our ministry, though manifested through different roles, has always been a shared endeavour. Our strengths complement each other, allowing us to cater to diverse needs within the community.

The success of our shared ministry lies in our united vision, solid commitment, and the grace of God guiding us every step of the way.

Navigating Ministry and Marriage

The early conversations between my husband and I set the foundation for our shared ministry. The prerequisite was clear: we both had to respect each other's callings. I was clear with my husband: I did not want to just be a housewife or his secretary; I wanted to continue pursuing what God had called me to do. And he understood. Before our marriage, we had a candid discussion about our expectations, roles, and responsibilities, ensuring that we were on the same page.

1. Communication is Key

One of the biggest lessons we have learned as a couple in ministry is the importance of communication. Physical distance does not matter as much as being emotionally distant does. Whether it is updating each other on our day, discussing ministry plans, or just checking in, we have made it a point to communicate regularly. We've also established rituals, like our family time when the children come home from school. These small moments of connection are invaluable.

2. Juggling Ministry and Family

Balancing ministry and family is indeed a challenge. But it is all about prioritising. When the children need us, that is where our attention goes. We ensure that we were present for those little moments, like when they come home from school eager to share their day. These moments might seem trivial but are crucial in making our children feel seen, heard, and loved.

3. Supporting Each Other

Our roles in ministry often mean one of us is travelling while the other is at home. But instead of seeing this as a challenge, we have turned it into an advantage. The one at home often takes over logistical tasks, like booking flights or making hotel arrangements, allowing the travelling partner to focus solely on the ministry. This mutual support system ensures neither of us feels overwhelmed and that the ministry is not compromised.

4. Taking Inspiration from Biblical Couples

Indeed, the Bible provides examples of couples who ministered together, such as Aquila and Priscilla. They served alongside the Apostle Paul, supporting him in his mission work. Their shared commitment to the cause of Christ is a shining example for couples like us. Their roles, though different, were complementary, echoing the synergy my husband and I strive for in our ministry.

Ministry, when done in pairs, has its own set of challenges. But with understanding, communication, and mutual support, it can be a fulfilling journey. For couples considering a shared ministry or simply striving for harmony in their relationship, remember that it is not about being perfect, but about being there for each other, communicating, and most importantly, keeping God at the centre of it all.

Chapter 9

Growing Storms

Life, much like the ever-changing weather, is unpredictable and can suddenly present us with challenges that resemble fierce storms. These storms, whether they are emotional, health-related, financial, or spiritual, are inevitable. However, it is not the storm that defines us, but how we respond to it. These challenges, or "growing storms" as I like to term them, are not mere disruptions or disturbances. They are, in fact, opportunities - opportunities to grow in faith, trust, and understanding of who we are and who we are with.

"*When you pass through the waters, I will be with you; and when you pass through the rivers, they will not sweep over you. When you walk through the fire, you will not be burned; the flames will not set you ablaze.*" Isaiah 43:2 (NIV)

As the Bible says, as we navigate our life's journey, it is essential to remember that we are never alone. Even in the fiercest of storms, Jesus is right there with us, guiding, protecting, and reassuring. The key is to remain focused on Him, for in Him lies our strength to endure and overcome. Remember, it is not about the storm; it is about who's in the boat with you.

Correction Storm

Correction storms arise when we stray from the path that God has set for us. Just like a loving parent who corrects their child to protect them from harm, God sometimes uses storms to bring our focus back to Him and His Divine plan. These storms, though challenging, are meant to draw us closer to Him and refine our character.

"Those whom I love, I rebuke and discipline. So be earnest and repent." Revelation 3:19 (NIV)

The story of Jonah is a powerful example of this. Jonah, a prophet of God, was instructed to go to Nineveh but chose to flee in the opposite direction. His disobedience led to a fierce storm that endangered not only his life but also the lives of those aboard the ship with him. It took being swallowed by a giant fish for Jonah to come to terms with his disobedience and seek God's mercy.

When faced with a correction storm, it is essential to self-reflect and evaluate whether we are in alignment with God's will. Just as Jonah's storm led him to repentance and eventually to fulfil God's mission in Nineveh, our correction storms can also lead us back to our Divine purpose. It is a reminder that God's plans for us are always for our good, even when we cannot see it. Embracing the storm and seeking God's direction can transform a correction storm into a season of growth and renewed purpose.

Growing Knowledge Storm

Growing knowledge storms serve to deepen our understanding and relationship with God. These storms are not necessarily punishments but rather situations or experiences that help us grow closer to God. They challenge our faith, our perceptions, and our understanding of who God is. Through these storms, we begin to see God not just as a distant deity but as an ever-present help and guide in our lives.

"He got up, rebuked the wind and said to the waves, 'Quiet! Be still!' Then the wind died down and it was completely calm. He said to his disciples, 'Why are you so afraid? Do you still have no faith?'" Mark 4:39-40 (NIV)

The account of Jesus calming the storm in Matthew 8:23 is a vivid representation of this. The disciples were on the boat with Jesus, yet they panicked when the storm hit. It is interesting to note that while they knew Jesus was with them, their focus was on the raging storm rather than the Saviour in their midst. Jesus' rebuke was not just about their lack of faith in Him to calm the storm, but also an invitation for them to know Him more deeply.

In our lives, growing knowledge storms will come, but they are opportunities to trust God more and to know Him more intimately. They remind us to shift our focus from the challenges we face to the One who has power over every storm. These storms are not meant to drown us but to elevate our understanding of who God is and how He operates in our lives. So, when you find yourself in the midst of a growing knowledge storm, remember to look to Jesus, trust in His power, and let the experience deepen your relationship and understanding of Him.

Miracle Storm

Miracle storms are unique in nature. They arise unexpectedly, often when we believe we are walking in obedience or when we are serving God passionately. Their purpose is not to punish or correct, but rather to manifest God's glory, power, and sovereignty in situations that seem impossible.

"Last night an angel of the God to whom I belong and whom I serve stood beside me and said, 'Do not be afraid, Paul. You must stand trial before Caesar; and God has graciously given you the lives of all who sail with you.'" Acts 27:23-24 (NIV)

The account in Acts 27 of Paul's shipwreck is a quintessential representation of this storm. Paul, a prisoner en route to Rome, finds himself amidst a violent storm. Despite his warnings, the crew faces dire circumstances. Yet, it is in this dire situation that Paul stands firm, not just in his faith, but in the specific word God gave him - that not a single life aboard the ship would be lost. The result? An entire shipwrecked crew witnesses the miraculous power of God, and Paul's prophetic word comes to pass. Similarly, your personal story of being scammed and then receiving not just restitution but more than what was taken from you is a testament to how God can turn situations around for His glory.

In the midst of miracle storms, it is essential to hold on to the promises of God and trust in His sovereignty. While the storm rages, it might seem like God is silent or has abandoned us. However, He often uses these situations to show us, and others, His might and power in ways we could never have imagined. Just as Paul's faith was a beacon of hope to the ship's crew and your restored finances testified to God's faithfulness, miracle storms are God's way of revealing Himself to us and those around us. Always remember, in the midst of the storm, God is preparing a miracle that will not only bless you but will also serve as a testimony to many.

Where Is The Storm Coming From?

The question often arises in the hearts of believers when they face challenges and trials: Where is this problem coming from? Is it divinely orchestrated, or is it an attack from the enemy?

Is it coming from God? The Bible makes it clear that God is not the author of confusion or problems. James 1:13 (ESV) says, "*Let no one say when he is tempted, 'I am being tempted by God,' for God cannot be tempted with evil, and he himself tempts no one.*" God does not create problems for us for the sake of testing or growing our faith.

Is it from the enemy but allowed by God? Yes, many challenges come from the enemy, as seen in the story of Job. Satan challenges Job's faith, but God permits it, knowing Job's character and faith. God does not bring the problem, but He might allow some problems to arise. Not because He wants to harm us, but because He trusts that we can endure and grow through it. As it is often said, "God will not give you more than you can handle." This aligns with 1 Corinthians 10:13 (ESV), which states, "*No temptation has overtaken you that is not common to man. God is faithful, and he will not let you be tempted beyond your ability, but with the temptation, he will also provide the way of escape, that you may be able to endure it.*"

Consider baking a cake. The baker knows precisely the temperature and the time required for the cake to be perfect. If baked too long or at too high a temperature, the cake will burn. Similarly, God, our creator, knows our limits. He knows exactly how much pressure, challenge, or heat we can endure without being destroyed.

While it may feel like God is silent during these storms, He is very much present and actively working for our good. In every situation, we can learn and grow. For instance, during an illness, one might learn the value of health and the importance of self-care. Our bodies are temples, as mentioned in 1 Corinthians 6:19, and we must take care of them.

In every storm, remember that God is faithful. He is with us, strengthening us, and He will always provide a way out. While the storms of life can be challenging, they also serve as invaluable lessons that deepen our faith, trust, and relationship with God.

Chapter 10

Wilderness Experience

In the heart of every believer, there is a vast expanse, a wilderness, where the soul is tested and refined. It is an unfamiliar terrain, often marked by isolation, trials, and temptations. But it is also a place of profound transformation.

"He led you through the vast and dreadful wilderness, that thirsty and waterless land, with its venomous snakes and scorpions. He brought you water out of hard rock." Deuteronomy 8:15 (NIV)

The concept of the 'wilderness experience' is deeply embedded in biblical history. It represents a period of trial, testing, and transition. It is not a punishment, but rather a purification process, designed to draw us closer to God, stripping away the distractions and attachments of the world.

Every believer who aspires to be more than just that - to be a true disciple of Christ - will, at some point, find themselves in this wilderness. It is almost a rite of passage in our spiritual journey. Not every believer will choose this path because it demands a deeper commitment, a willingness to be refined, and a desire to grow closer to God.

Jesus Himself was not exempt from this. After the Divine affirmation at His baptism, where the heavens opened, and God proclaimed Him as His beloved Son, Jesus was led by the Spirit into the wilderness. Before He performed any miracle, before He preached any sermon, He faced the wilderness. There, He fasted for 40 days and nights, confronting the temptations of the flesh and the devil.

This wilderness experience is a reminder that our spiritual journey is not always about mountaintop experiences or miraculous moments. Sometimes, it is about enduring the testing times, holding onto faith when the path is not clear, and relying on God's word when our flesh wants to lead us astray.

As disciples, our journey through the wilderness is essential. It is here that we learn to discern the voice of God from our feelings, to differentiate between the Holy Spirit's guidance and our own desires. It is a time to lean into God, to be fortified in His Word, and to emerge stronger, ready to step into our calling and purpose.

Lessons from the Wilderness

The wilderness experience is a profound stage in a believer's journey to becoming a disciple. It is a rite of passage, a test, a refining fire where the fleshly desires are confronted head-on, and the spirit is schooled in the ways of God. Misinterpretations and false prophecies stem from a place where the flesh is still alive and unchecked, where emotions and personal desires cloud the true voice of God. Hence, one must learn to differentiate between personal feelings and the genuine prompting of the Spirit.

Jesus, in His earthly ministry, was not exempt from this process. The devil, seizing on His physical hunger after 40 days of fasting, tempted Him with the very basics: bread. The taunt, “If you are the Son of God”, aimed to cast doubt and appeal to pride. How many times in our lives are we faced with situations where we think, “I have the authority or the means, so why should not I just do this?” It is a delicate balance between acknowledging God’s gifts and blessings, like a six-month visa, and not acting out of our own will or presumption.

The wilderness is a place of desolation, hunger, and thirst. Yet, it is also where God’s voice becomes crystal clear, where distractions are minimal, and where reliance on Him is absolute. John the Baptist chose this environment to remain unblemished from societal influences, ensuring his message remained pure. His boldness in confronting King Herod about his sinful relationship was not because John was fearless, but because he was clear about God's message.

As ministers or disciples, the wilderness experience prepares us for the challenges ahead. It teaches us to stand firm, even when faced with criticism or unpopularity. It is not about appeasing everyone; it is about delivering God's truth, even if it is uncomfortable. And when we understand that our sustenance does not come from bread alone but from every word that God speaks, we are better equipped to face life's challenges.

Jesus' confrontation on the temple's pinnacle reminds us that while knowledge of the scripture is commendable, its correct application is crucial. The devil knows the scripture too, but his interpretations are always twisted. We are reminded that our spiritual journey is not just about consumption (reading and memorising the Word) but more about application (living it out). If natural bread has the power to give life to the living, why cannot it revive a dead man? This shows that man cannot truly live by bread alone but needs every word that comes from God.

Temptations in the Wilderness

False prophecies arise because, often, we do not differentiate between our feelings and our flesh. The wilderness experience is a powerful lesson on this. When Jesus was in the wilderness, tempted by the devil, He showcased the strength of spirit over flesh. The devil challenged him, saying, "If you are the Son of God, command these stones to become bread." This is a temptation many face in service to the Lord. For instance, sometimes we might think that because of a particular blessing or 'visa' in our life, we can stay in a comfort zone a bit longer. But this is not always in line with God's will; it is often just our own desires or flesh speaking.

Many ministries begin with great zeal and purpose, but over time, as they grow and face the temptations of the wilderness - loneliness, dryness, hunger - they lose their way. It is in the wilderness, though, that God's voice becomes clearest.

Take the life of John the Baptist, for instance. He chose solitude in the wilderness over societal comforts, which gave him the boldness to confront a king about his sins. This boldness stems from a deep connection with God, a clarity that is not clouded by societal norms or fears.

This wilderness experience is not just about physical needs or our five senses. It is primarily about tuning in to the Word of God. For if natural bread gives life to people, why cannot it revive the dead? This underlines the truth that we do not live by bread alone but by every word that comes from God.

The second temptation Jesus faced was when the devil dared him to jump off the temple's pinnacle, quoting scripture to back his challenge. This teaches us an essential lesson. Knowing God's word is not enough; we must apply it rightly. Using scripture for personal gain or to test God is a wrong application.

In our service to the Lord, it is not about personal fame

or gain. It is about Him. The Lord once revealed to me the essence of being "faceless" and "nameless" - it is not about our glory but His. If we seek to elevate ourselves, we are, in essence, stealing from God's glory.

The journey in the wilderness is filled with trials and tests. For instance, my husband was once offered a prestigious position with the UN, but when they restricted him from sharing the gospel, he declined. The offer was tempting, with many worldly comforts attached. But the essence of our calling is not about these comforts or recognitions. It is about serving God wholeheartedly and aligning with His will, even if it means facing the challenges of the wilderness.

Overcoming Temptations

In the huge area of the wilderness, we often confront the core essence of our faith and service. It is not about entertaining ourselves or seeking personal glory. As Jesus emphasised, our purpose is not for our kingdom but for His (Matthew 4:1-11).

Throughout His time in the wilderness, Jesus faced multiple temptations from Satan. One was the temptation to turn stones into bread, which tested His physical needs versus spiritual obedience. Another was to throw Himself from the pinnacle of the temple, challenging Him to test God's protection. The last was when Satan offered Him all the kingdoms of the world if Jesus would worship him. Each time, Jesus responded with the Word of God, showcasing the importance of knowing and applying scripture in our lives.

Many times, without realising it, we may find ourselves stealing God's glory and adjusting it to fit our narrative. We might be swayed by worldly allurements and power, tempted to worship the world, our congregations, or even our challenges. Especially during trying times when we feel isolated and defeated, Satan attempts to derail our destiny (John 10:10).

However, the wilderness experience teaches us several key lessons:

1. **Our Identity in Christ**: The devil often questioned Jesus, saying, "If you are the Son of God". This mirrors the doubts and questions we might face about our faith. But the wilderness solidifies our identity. We are not just believers asking God for things but disciples serving Him, embracing the responsibilities and privileges that come with that identity.

2. **Serving the True Master**: In the wilderness, we learn about devotion and loyalty. If we truly are children of God, our focus should be on serving the Father, not our desires or ambitions. As Jesus declared, *"I only do what I saw my father did"* (John 5:19). This highlights the heart of genuine ministry.

3. **Exercising Our Authority**: Jesus did not merely rebuke the devil with words; He used His Divine authority. Similarly, we have been given authority as children of God. We do not need to plead for our rights in His kingdom. Instead, we should command and declare, rooted in our identity and

His promises.

In essence, the wilderness is a refining fire, affirming our position in God's kingdom, the authority we carry, and how we should exercise it. It is not a place of defeat but a training ground, preparing us for greater works in His name. Remember, if we truly know who we are in Christ, the question is not about what we can do, but about obeying the Father's will.

Conclusion

Personal Invitation

As we conclude this transformative journey of *"Faith Unveiled"*, there lies an open invitation for each one of you. This is not just my story; it is an invitation to embark on your own personal encounter with God. Each page of this book has echoed a heart's desire, a hunger to truly know the God we worship, to move beyond rituals and traditions, and to forge a genuine, deep relationship with Him.

During a past summer, we hosted a one-week children's Bible camp catering to various age groups. Our days were filled with teachings on salvation and Christian living based on the Bible, while evenings were dedicated to praise, worship, and age-specific Bible studies. The camp was a success, with numerous children embracing the love of God and committing their lives to Him. Some underwent transformative changes, altering the way they lived and spoke while relinquishing worldly pleasures. However, an unexpected incident occurred on Saturday night when a young man from the camp invited all the children to his home, an hour's drive away. Unbeknownst to anyone, he exposed them to inappropriate content online, contrary to the values they had been taught throughout the week.

Upon learning of this in the morning, shock and confusion engulfed me. I felt a mixture of anger and concern, realising the potential dangers they had faced. The incident involved deception by a youth leader, unauthorised outing, and a stark deviation from the lessons learned during the week. As the children admitted their wrongdoing, confessing before God and all the parents and adults, a profound lesson on sin, punishment, God's grace, and forgiveness unfolded. Reflecting on this, I considered the story of Adam and Eve in the Garden of Eden, recognising how deception can lead to the destruction of the blessings God provides.

Drawing on theological insights, I acknowledged the importance of emphasising sin and its consequences more seriously, prioritising the demonstration of God's love and forgiveness over punitive measures. In Romans 5:1-18, the passage illustrates that though sin entered the world through one man, the righteousness of Christ justifies all. Despite the seeming power of sin, the forgiveness of sin holds greater strength.

Throughout the Bible camp, children were taught about God's love, forgiveness, sin, and its consequences. While they gained head knowledge, it was when faced with the reality of temptation, committing sin, and expecting punishment that the profound impact of total forgiveness became evident. Understanding the love of God, the significance of repentance, and the transformative power of forgiveness became a reality for them.

This incident reinforced the practicality of theology in our daily lives. When we forgive one another and confess our sins, God is ever-ready to extend His forgiveness. As we forgave the children for their admitted wrongs, it became clear how theology transcends theoretical concepts to shape our day-to-day experiences.

In light of the lessons learned from this impactful experience, let us not only contemplate the theology of forgiveness but also embrace it in our own lives. Just as those children admitted their wrongs and found forgiveness, we too can turn to Christ, acknowledging our own shortcomings. In the face of sin and its consequences, Christ offers total forgiveness and transformation. Let this be an invitation to each heart, urging us to accept Christ's forgiveness, to experience the love and grace that can redeem and renew us. As we reflect on God's boundless mercy, may it inspire a personal journey towards Christ, seeking His forgiveness, and allowing His love to shape our lives.

Growing up, I felt the weight of religious practices that seemed empty without understanding the essence. I yearned for a tangible experience with God, not just a second-hand faith borrowed from my parents. I took a step back, seeking an authentic encounter, and the living God did not disappoint. Just as Zacchaeus in the Bible was called out by Jesus who knew him by name even before their meeting, I felt God calling me. He knows each one of us intimately, even before we seek Him.

If there is a burning desire within you to truly know and experience God, I assure you, He will make a way. My journey, filled with miracles, personal counsel from Jesus, and profound spiritual growth, is testament to that. But it does not stop there. Our walk with God is sustained by the Holy Spirit, our Comforter, who guides, teaches, and reveals the depths of God's character to us. Embracing the Holy Spirit is paramount for a fulfilling Christian life.

Yes, the journey has its challenges – storms that test our

faith, wilderness periods that refine our character – but they are not setbacks. They are growth opportunities, shaping us to understand God as our Provider, our Sustainer, and our Protector. Psalm 121 reminds us that our help comes from the Lord, the Maker of heaven and earth. In the midst of our trials, He remains steadfast.

So, dear reader, if you have been inspired by this book, share it. Encourage others to get into these pages, to seek their personal encounter with God. And if you have been searching for a deeper, more genuine relationship with Him, this is your moment. Seek Him wholeheartedly. Yearn for the Holy Spirit's guidance. For in that earnest seeking, you will find a God who is very much alive, personal, and eager to journey with you.

In the end, it is not just about reading a story; it is about living your own story of transformation and faith. God awaits your call. Will you answer?

About The Author

The Revd. Dr. Huai Man Cing Hatzaw is a Baptist ordained minister, ordained by the Zomi Baptist Convention of Myanmar and the Baptist Union of Great Britain. She was born in 1963 in Falam, Chin State, Myanmar (Burma). Though brought up in a disciplined family, she did not embrace a genuine Christian life initially. She was sceptical about faith and Christianity until she experienced spiritual rebirth in May 1981. Since her conversion, she has faithfully and wholeheartedly followed Jesus in all aspects of her life. In the same year (1981), she received a divine call from God to serve in Christian ministry, to which she was strongly determined.

Responding to this lifelong calling, she began studying theology at the Burma Institute of Theology (B.I.T, now M.I.T) in Yangon, Myanmar, for her B. Th. She furthered her studies at Zomi Theological College, Falam, Chin State, Myanmar, earning her B. R. E. She married Gin Khan Khual in 1990. For her husband's doctoral studies at the University of Glasgow, Scotland, the family relocated from Myanmar to the UK in 1998. During their time in Scotland, she pursued her B. A. in Theology at International Christian College, Glasgow, and her M. Th. at the University of Glasgow. Upon the family's move to England in 2003, she completed her M. Th. in Applied Theology at Oxford University. Finally, she earned her Doctor of Counselling from the University of Christian Leadership in the United States of America in 2021.

Her Christian ministry began as a Pastor in her hometown of Tedim, Chin State, in 1988. She later served with Youth With A Mission in India in 1989 and gained teaching experience in theological colleges in Tedim, Falam, and Glasgow, Scotland. Renowned as a conference speaker in the UK and other countries, she is passionately committed to evangelism, both locally and globally. Additionally, she is well-known for her counselling and life coaching expertise.

Currently residing in Oxford, England, with her husband and four grown children, she pastors the Burmese Mission Church in Oxford and actively participates in Worldwide Evangelism Mission, her husband Gin Khan Khual's God-given vision for global gospel outreach.

Printed in Great Britain
by Amazon

42144152R00106